CULTURES OF THE WORLD
Azerbaijan

Cavendish
Square
New York

Published in 2021 by Cavendish Square Publishing, LLC
243 5th Avenue, Suite 136, New York, NY 10016
Copyright © 2021 by Cavendish Square Publishing, LLC

Third Edition

Library of Congress Cataloging-in-Publication Data

Names: King, David C., author. | Nevins, Debbie, author.
Title: Azerbaijan / David C. King and Debbie Nevins.
Description: Third edition. | New York : Cavendish Square Publishing, 2021.
 | Series: Cultures of the world | Includes bibliographical references
 and index.
Identifiers: LCCN 2020020203 | ISBN 9781502658708 (library binding) | ISBN
 9781502658715 (ebook)
Subjects: LCSH: Azerbaijan--Juvenile literature.
Classification: LCC DK692.3 .K56 2021 | DDC 947.54--dc23
LC record available at https://lccn.loc.gov/2020020203

Writers, third edition: David C. King; Debbie Nevins
Editor, third edition: Debbie Nevins
Designer, third edition: Jessica Nevins
Picture Researcher, third edition: Jessica Nevins

PICTURE CREDITS

The photographs in this book are used with the permission of: Cover; p. 1 gfarique/Shutterstock.com; p. 3 moviephoto/Shutterstock.com; pp. 5, 9, 41 ET1972/Shutterstock.com; p. 6 Cartarium/Shutterstock.com; p. 7 Emad aljumah/Moment/Getty Images; pp. 8, 19, 68 Viktor Loki/Shutterstock.com; p. 10 mbrand85/Shutterstock.com; pp. 12, 103 (top), 104 saiko3p/Shutterstock.com; pp. 13, 15 Rainer Lesniewski/Shutterstock.com; p. 14 tour-de-segur/Shutterstock.com; pp. 16, 52, 63, 86 Vastram/Shutterstock.com; p. 17 Iryna Savina/Shutterstock.com; p. 18 Limpopo/Shutterstock.com; p. 20 Boris Stroujko/Shutterstock.com; pp. 21, 54 IanRedding/Shutterstock.com; p. 22 Jiri Fejkl/Shutterstock.com; p. 23 2TRL Media/Shutterstock.com; p. 24 Damian Pankowiec/Shutterstock.com; p. 26 In Green/Shutterstock.com; p. 29 Universal History Archive/Getty Images; p. 31 aquatarkus/Shutterstock.com; pp. 32, 55, 80 Reza/Getty Images; p. 33 knovakov/Shutterstock.com; p. 34 Azerbaijani Presidency/Handout/Anadolu Agency/Getty Images; p. 36 Felix Lipov/Shutterstock.com; p. 40 PHILIPPE WOJAZER/AFP via Getty Images; p. 44 Janusz Pienkowski/Shutterstock.com; pp. 46, 92 Ana Flasker/Shutterstock.com; p. 48 vuqarali/Shutterstock.com; p. 50 Ovchinnikova Irina/Shutterstock.com; p. 56 Barta28/Shutterstock.com; p. 57 Agami Photo Agency/Shutterstock.com; p. 58 (top) Rostislav Stefanek/Shutterstock.com; p. 58 (bottom) Negro Elkha/Shutterstock.com; p. 60 Alizada Studios/Shutterstock.com; p. 62 AlizadaStudios/iStock Editorial/Getty Images Plus; p. 64 Lyokin/Shutterstock.com; p. 65 tenkl/Shutterstock.com; p. 66 Oleksandr Rupeta/NurPhoto via Getty Images; p. 70 Borka Kiss/Shutterstock.com; p. 72 Tatsiana Hendzel/Shutterstock.com; p. 75 Dilara Mammadova/Shutterstock.com; p. 76 Ungvari Attila/Shutterstock.com; pp. 79, 100 Photographer RM/Shutterstock.com; p. 83 RAMNIKLAL MODI/Shutterstock.com; p. 84 Resul Rehimov/Anadolu Agency via Getty Images; p. 88 Hadrian/Shutterstock.com; p. 94 posztos/Shutterstock.com; pp. 95, 111 Kaliam/Shutterstock.com; p. 97 -/AFP via Getty Images; p. 98 Retan/Shutterstock.com; p. 99 Ansis Klucis/Shutterstock.com; p. 101 alisafarov/Shutterstock.com; p. 102 Kirill Skorobogatko/Shutterstock.com; p. 103 (middle), 108 Adil Celebiyev/Shutterstock.com; p. 103 (bottom) leshiy985/Shutterstock.com; p. 106 alexsaz/Shutterstock.com; p. 109 Rzaev/Shutterstock.com; pp. 112, 126, 130 Eldar Farz/Shutterstock.com; p. 114 Seljan Gurbanova/Shutterstock.com; p. 116 Torabora641/Shutterstock.com; p. 117 Elena Odareeva/Shutterstock.com; p. 119 vuqarali/Shutterstock.com; p. 120 Denis Sv/Shutterstock.com; p. 122 Genc Subhan/Shutterstock.com; p. 125 moonnoor/Shutterstock.com; p. 127 k_samurkas/Shutterstock.com; p. 128 turtle_stock/Shutterstock.com; p. 131 AnikonaAnn/Shutterstock.com; p. 137 Kypros/Moment/Getty Images.

Some of the images in this book illustrate individuals who are models. The depictions do not imply actual situations or events.

CPSIA compliance information: Batch #CW21CSQ: For further information contact Cavendish Square Publishing LLC, New York, New York, at 1-877-980-4450.

Printed in the United States of America

Find us on

CONTENTS

AZERBAIJAN TODAY

WHAT COUNTRY LIES EAST OF EUROPE, WEST OF ASIA, NORTH of the Middle East, and south of Russia? Here are some hints, or perhaps they are riddles: This place lies between two seas and across jagged mountains. Its mountains are full of snow, but its soil is full of fire. Its arteries flow with oil and gas, but its volcanoes spew mud. This is a landlocked country, but its capital city embraces a sea. Leaping above that city's skyline are towering flames. At night, they glow in blazing colors—for this country calls itself the Land of Fire.

The Flame Towers are skyscrapers, the city is Baku, the sea is the Caspian, and the country is Azerbaijan. Its name means "land of fire." A country of contrasts and contradictions, it is at once very old and very new. Geographically and culturally, it is a nation between competing influences. The country straddles two continents, with one foot in Europe and the other in Asia. Culturally, it does very much the same thing, with the added Persian influence of the Middle East. Historically, it's linked to Russia, having spent around 70 years as a Soviet republic.

Azerbaijan is a majority Muslim country that is proudly secular. It's a republic, but its people are not really free—at least, not according to numerous international human rights organizations. Azerbaijan claims to be a peaceful nation, yet it's in a constant state of discord with its neighbor Armenia. These are just some of the conflicting characteristics of this land.

Azerbaijan is one of three independent nations in Transcaucasia; the other two are Georgia and Armenia. Transcaucasia, named for the Caucasus Mountains, is an expanse of land that lies between the Black Sea and the Caspian Sea. Azerbaijan is on the eastern side, bordering the Caspian—a great inland sea with no outlet to the earth's oceans, which makes Azerbaijan technically landlocked. The country's most densely populated region is a small peninsular hook of land that extends into this sea. Beneath the land and the sea lie treasure—the oil and natural gas that fuel the country's economy as well as the strange fire phenomena that give Azerbaijan its name.

Azerbaijan is made up of a number of pieces that fit together like a puzzle. This puzzle has two pieces, or perhaps three. The main piece of the nation

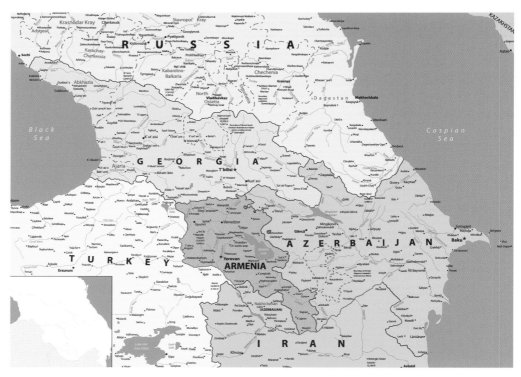

This map shows the Caucasus region, with Azerbaijan and its neighbors as well as the Black Sea and the Caspian Sea.

is separated from its western exclave, the Naxcivan Autonomous Republic (sometimes spelled Nakhichevan), by a stretch of Armenian land. Adding to the confusion is yet another autonomous region, Nagorno-Karabakh. This puzzle piece is claimed by Azerbaijan, but it is also the self-proclaimed nation of Artsakh, made up of ethnic Armenians. This disputed territory is a very sore spot for Azerbaijan—an open wound that won't heal. Despite a 1994 ceasefire, and numerous international attempts at a peace settlement, violence still flares up on its borders.

Since it first became an independent nation in 1991, Azerbaijan's status in the world has risen. It has redefined itself as a major regional energy supplier, which has increased its wealth and influence. Pipelines crisscross the country, delivering gas and oil to energy-hungry Europe. The profits have helped develop the country's infrastructure as the economy has grown. [Note: The

Stepanakert is the capital of the Republic of Artsakh, or the largest city in Azerbaijan's Nagorno-Karabakh region, depending on one's perspective. The city lies on the Karabakh Plateau at an average altitude of 2,667 feet (813 meters).

A multitude of rigs drill for oil in a large, flat field in Azerbaijan.

economic information in this book does not reflect the effects of the 2020 global coronavirus pandemic, which at this writing remain to be determined.]

All that good news is dampened, however, by international concerns about corruption. The government is accused of growing authoritarianism. The country's leadership has remained in the Aliyev family since Heydar Aliyev became president in 1993 and was succeeded by his son, Ilham, in 2003. As president, Ilham Aliyev is behaving more and more like a dictator. He has managed to have the constitution changed to his benefit several times, allowing him to rule indefinitely and with ever-increasing power. In particular, he has quashed political opposition and clamped down on civil liberties. Journalists are especially restricted. Many have been detained or imprisoned on fabricated charges, while others face travel bans.

Despite that menacing shadow, Azerbaijan is a land of striking beauty and variety. Its many regions include the snowcapped peaks of the Greater

The Philharmonic Fountain Park is located near the ancient walls of the Old City in Baku.

Caucasus Mountains, fertile river valleys interlaced with irrigation canals, subtropical forests, and tea plantations in the south. In contrast, arid patches of semi-desert are found near the Caspian Sea. In places, Azerbaijan looks like a country forgotten by time. Ancient churches and mosques rise above medieval villages or the walled "old town" areas of cities. In other places, definite signs of the 21st century emerge in the glass-and-steel office buildings of modern urban centers.

Each year, more tourists flock to the country to discover its wonders, a trend that also helps to grow the economy. What lies ahead for paradoxical Azerbaijan? Like the country itself, the answer is a mystery.

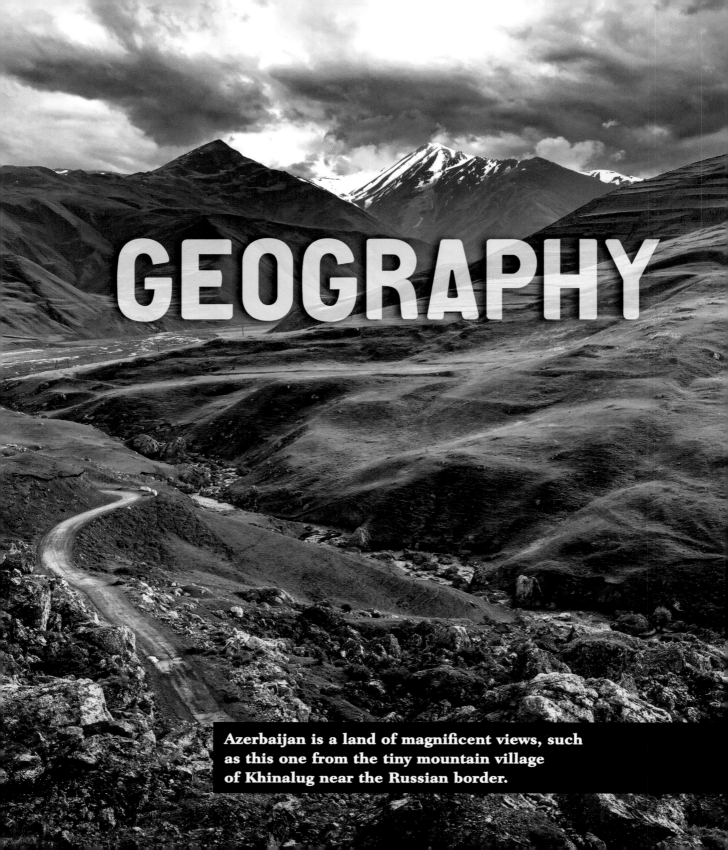

GEOGRAPHY

Azerbaijan is a land of magnificent views, such as this one from the tiny mountain village of Khinalug near the Russian border.

AZERBAIJAN IS A COUNTRY ON THE dividing line between Europe and Asia. Most of it falls in southwestern Asia, with a small northern portion resting in Europe. The line between Europe and Asia is an imaginary line, created by geographers, so there is no actual geographical divide.

With a combined land and water area of 33,436 square miles (86,600 square kilometers), the nation is roughly the size of the state of Maine—but more irregularly shaped. The Greater Caucasus Mountains form Azerbaijan's northern border with Russia, while the Caspian Sea marks the eastern boundary. Although the country has coastline on the Caspian, it is still considered a landlocked nation. That's because it has no access to the oceans.

To the west of Azerbaijan lie Armenia and Georgia, which were also former republics of the Soviet Union. In the south, the Aras River (or Araks) and the Talysh, or Talish, Mountains separate Azerbaijan from Iran.

The country is dominated by spectacular mountain ranges, yet more than 40 percent of Azerbaijan is low flatlands. A large portion of these lowlands is made up of arid semi-desert, but irrigation makes nearly half of the total land area suitable for farming. The mild climate combined with extensive irrigation has enabled Azerbaijan to be a major food producer. Until the Soviet Union collapsed in the early 1990s, the republic accounted for about 10 percent of the entire Soviet agricultural output.

1

Transcaucasia is a geographical area in the southern Caucasus Mountain region on the border of eastern Europe and western Asia. It roughly corresponds to the area of today's Georgia, Armenia, and Azerbaijan. It extends from the Black Sea in the west to the Caspian Sea in the east. To the north of this region is Russia, and to the south, are Turkey and Iran.

The jagged peaks of the Greater Caucasus Mountains mark the highest parts of Azerbaijan.

GEOGRAPHIC REGIONS

Roughly half the country is mountainous, dominated by the towering northern peaks of the Greater Caucasus Mountains. Azerbaijan's highest peaks are located there, including Mount Bazarduzu (Bazarduzu Dagi) at 14,652 feet (4,466 m). The jagged peaks and glaciers of the high mountains offer breathtaking views of the lower valleys, where rushing streams thread through spectacular gorges.

The fertile lower slopes of the mountains are covered with forests interspersed with pastureland. In the extreme northeast, however, the foothills lack the same rich, well-watered soil and give way to an arid coastal plain on the edge of the Caspian Sea.

To the south and west, the rugged Lesser Caucasus Mountains form a second important mountain system. In this region, the disputed territory of

NAGORNO-KARABAKH

The geographic area of Azerbaijan includes the breakaway republic of Nagorno-Karabakh in the western part of the country. Although it is internationally recognized as a part of Azerbaijan, it is a disputed territory and a de facto (in reality) independent state made up mostly of ethnic Armenians. It has not been governed by Azerbaijan since 1988, when war broke out between Azerbaijan and Armenia, lasting until a 1994 ceasefire. The dispute remains unresolved.

This map shows Azerbaijan in green and the disputed Nagorno-Karabakh area in yellow.

Nagorno-Karabakh is located. Bordering the peaks is the Kura River depression, a series of plains and low hills separated by the Kura and Aras Rivers. This is the lowest region of Azerbaijan, and much of it lies below sea level. In the central and eastern areas of the depression, the soil is enriched by the annual deposits of silt as the Kura empties into the Caspian Sea.

The 443-mile (713 km) coastline on the Caspian has few bays or inlets. The three largest projections of land into the sea are the Absheron Peninsula (Absheron Yasaqligi), on which the capital city of Baku is situated; the Sara Peninsula; and the Kura Sandbar.

RIVERS AND LAKES

There are more than 1,000 rivers in Azerbaijan, but only about 20 are longer than 60 miles (97 km). The Kura River is by far the largest—in fact, it's the largest in all of Transcaucasia. It flows from northwest to southeast and empties into the Caspian Sea. Most of the country's rivers are found in the lowlands between the Kura and Aras Rivers. In the south, the Aras River and the Talysh Mountains form the border between Azerbaijan and Iran.

The many rivers join an elaborate network of canals to irrigate large fields of cotton and grain. One major waterway is the Upper Karabakh Canal, which provides irrigation for its entire length of 107 miles (172 km), watering 250,000 acres (101,171 hectares) of farmland. The canal also feeds the

Bathers enjoy a public beach area in Azerbaijan.

THE LARGEST INLAND SEA-OR LAKE?

The Caspian Sea is the largest inland body of water in the world. It's much bigger than Lake Superior, the greatest of the North American Great Lakes, which is the second-largest inland body of water. For comparison, the Caspian measures about 750 miles (1,200 km) from north to south, and it's about 200 miles (322 km) wide. It covers around 149,200 square miles (386,426 sq km) in area. Lake Superior, in contrast, measures only 160 miles (258 km) from north to south, and it's 350 miles (563 km) from east to west. It covers 31,700 square miles (82,102 sq km).

This map shows the Caspian Sea and its surrounding countries.

Is the comparison even valid? Unlike Lake Superior or the other Great Lakes, the Caspian is not a freshwater body but a salt lake. Then there's its name—it's not Caspian Lake, after all, but the Caspian Sea. So which is it—a lake or a sea? As it turns out, that's a question geologists have long struggled with and never quite settled.

Around 11 million years ago—which is relatively recent in geologic time—the Caspian was linked to the ocean by way of the Sea of Azov, the Black Sea, the Aegean Sea, and the Mediterranean Sea. At that point, it was unquestionably a sea. However, over time, the rising landforms of Asia and Europe slowly isolated the saltwater Caspian in a large hollow that is around 72 feet (22 m) below sea level.

The depth of the sea varies greatly, from a shallow 12 feet to 20 feet (3.7 m to 6.1 m) in the north to a maximum depth of 3,360 feet (1,024 m). There is also wide variation in the water's salinity, or salt content. In the cooler north, where great Russian freshwater rivers such as the Volga and Vistula flow into the Caspian, the salt content is low. In the subtropical south, where evaporation occurs at a much faster rate, the salinity level is much higher. On average, the Caspian's salinity is about one-third that of ocean water.

Mingachevir Reservoir, a huge human-made lake. It covers 234 square miles (606 sq km) and has a maximum depth of about 246 feet (75 m). Built in 1953, it's the largest lake in Azerbaijan and the location of its largest hydroelectric power plant. The Upper Shirvan Canal, the second-most important canal, also irrigates around 250,000 acres (1,012 sq km) along its 75-mile (121-m) length.

Although there are around 450 lakes in Azerbaijan, they are all quite small. Most are freshwater, but some are saltwater. The largest natural lake is Sarysu ("Yellow Lake"), a very shallow body of water with an average depth of only 1.64 feet (0.5 m) and a maximum depth of almost 20 feet (6 m). One of the most beautiful places in the country is Lake Goygol ("Blue Lake"), a tourist favorite in the foothills of the Lesser Caucasus. The greater Goygol region actually contains a series of 19 lakes. The water is so clear that it's said one can easily see 26 feet to 33 feet (8 m to 10 m) below the surface. The Goygol Natural Park was established in this region in 2008, but it was preceded by a reserve that was created in 1925.

Lake Goygol was formed when an earthquake in 1139 caused a landslide off Mount Kapaz to block a river below. The resulting high-altitude lake is known for its beauty.

The Gobustan region of Azerbaijan is a hotbed of erupting mud. It's a place where geological processes produce a natural phenomenon known as mud volcanoes. In fact, Azerbaijan has the most mud volcanoes of any country—between 350 and 400 of them. These cone-like hills exude a mud-like substance that is formed deep below Earth's surface. Although

Mud oozes out of the peculiar volcanoes in Gobustan.

they are not true volcanoes in the sense that they don't produce lava, these ruptures in Earth's crust operate in a similar way.

Heated water and subterranean mineral deposits form a mud-like slurry, which is forced upward under pressure. Deep underground, gases heat up and ignite, sometimes sending flames into the air when the volcanoes erupt. Most mud volcanoes are much smaller than igneous volcanoes, and the mud that oozes or gushes out is not nearly as hot as magma. Some is quite cold. Some volcanoes produce a mud that is comfortably warm and people bathe in it for its purported health benefits.

CLIMATE

Most of Azerbaijan has a subtropical climate, but there is considerable variation across the country, depending on factors such as precipitation and altitude. Summers, for example, are generally warm and dry, particularly in the central and eastern parts of the country. Along the coast of the Caspian Sea, however, rainfall amounts to only 8 inches to 12 inches

NAXCIVAN: AN ISOLATED PROVINCE

Naxcivan is a small wedge of mountainous territory located between Armenia and Iran. (The spellings of this region's name vary—it is also referred to as Nakhchivan, Nakhichevan, and numerous other variations.) The region is an exclave of Azerbaijan. An exclave is a region that is geographically separated from the rest of its country by alien territory. In the case of Naxcivan, it is separated from Azerbaijan by at least 30 miles (48.3 km) of Armenian territory. Naxcivan is an autonomous republic, governed by its own legislature. Its administrative capital is the city of Naxcivan.

An arid plain reveals the stark desert beauty of Naxcivan.

About 400,000 people live in the exclave. The people are almost entirely Azerbaijanis, and it was their determination, with the support of the government in Azerbaijan's capital of Baku, that kept the exclave a part of Azerbaijan after the breakup of the Soviet Union in the early 1990s.

According to legend, this tiny region was founded before 1500 BCE by Noah, the biblical ark builder. It prospered under Persian rule in the Middle Ages, then was taken over by Russia in 1828, and became part of the Soviet Union. In January 1990, as the Soviet Union began to crumble, Naxcivan became the first part of the former Soviet Union to declare its independence. Within a few months, however, the people voted to become part of Azerbaijan.

Geographically, the exclave is primarily semi-desert terrain, extremely arid and mountainous, with a small region of plains. Agriculture in those flatlands, which includes the growing of grains and vegetables and the raising of cattle, is supported by irrigation. Valleys are speckled with orchards that produce apricots, pears, and peaches. The rocky mountainsides offer breathtaking views of nearby Iran, Armenia, and Nagorno-Karabakh.

(20.3 centimeters to 31 centimeters) per year, producing a semi-desert climate. Farther south, in an area called the Lankaran Lowland, rainfall is between 47 inches and 55 inches (119.4 cm and 140 cm) a year, which produces a more humid climate suitable for crops such as tea and cotton. There, in the extreme southeast, which lies below sea level, the summers are long—four to five months—and very hot, with temperatures averaging 81° Fahrenheit (27° Celsius) but often topping 100°F (38°C).

In other parts of the country, the climate varies a great deal with the altitude. In the foothills of the mountain ranges, temperatures are milder, and annual rainfall ranges from 12 inches to 35 inches (31 cm to 89 cm). The higher peaks of both the Lesser and Greater Caucasus ranges are in a mountain-forest zone, where low rainfall and summer temperatures averaging 41°F (5°C) produce tundra-like conditions—the kind of climate found in subarctic regions such as southern Alaska. At altitudes above 10,000 feet (3,048 m), cold temperatures and heavy snowfall keep the mountain passes closed for three or four months each year.

Sandstone hills rise over a desert landscape in Azerbaijan.

WORLD HERITAGE SITES

Since 1975, the United Nations Educational, Scientific, and Cultural Organization (UNESCO) has maintained a list of international landmarks or regions considered to be of "outstanding value" to the people of the world. Such sites embody the common natural and cultural heritage of humanity, and therefore deserve particular protection. The organization works with the host country to establish plans for managing and conserving the sites. UNESCO also reports on sites that are in imminent or potential danger of destruction and can offer emergency funds to try to save the site.

The organization is continually assessing new sites for inclusion on the World Heritage List. In order to be selected, a site must be of "outstanding universal value" and meet at least one of ten criteria. These required elements include cultural value—that is, artistic, religious, or historical significance—and natural value, including exceptional beauty, unusual natural phenomenon, and scientific importance.

As of June 2020, there were 1,121 sites listed: 869 cultural, 213 natural, and 39 mixed (cultural and natural) properties in 167 nations. Of those, 53 are listed as "in danger."

Azerbaijan has three cultural sites and no natural ones as of 2020. The three sites are the Gobustan Rock Art Cultural Landscape; the Historic Center of Sheki

with the Khan's Palace; and the Walled City of Baku with the Shirvanshahs' Palace and Maiden Tower (shown here, with the Flame Towers in the background). The country has submitted nine more properties for World Heritage consideration, and they are on the Tentative List.

FLORA AND FAUNA

Variations in altitude and climate create wide differences in plant and animal life. More than 4,000 species of plants are found in Azerbaijan. The semi-desert conditions of the lowlands and the drier foothills of some mountain ranges support a variety of grasses and shrubs. Large areas of forest cover the southern slopes of the Greater Caucasus, parts of the Lesser Caucasus, and the Talysh Mountains. These lush forests are home to Iberian oaks, beeches, eastern birches, albizzias, and ironwoods.

Azerbaijan has a rich variety of animal life, with more than 12,000 species. In the lowlands, herds of gazelles graze the semi-desert grasses, avoiding packs of jackals and hyenas. These arid regions are also home to many species of snakes and rodents. In the Kura-Aras Valley and on the mountain slopes, roe deer and Caucasian deer are numerous, sharing their habitat with wild boars, lynx, brown bears, chamois, mountain goats (at higher elevations), and occasionally leopards.

A collared dwarf snake *(Eirenis collaris)* lies coiled at rest on the ground near Baku.

There are also a few herds of European bison, or wisents. These shaggy creatures look much like North American bison and are actually a little larger. Like many other big-game species, wisents were overhunted—mostly in the 17th and 18th centuries—and by the mid-1900s, the species was close to extinction. Most of the remaining herds are now protected in game preserves and parks.

The mild winters lure many flocks of birds to the shores of the Caspian Sea, and nature reserves offer a safe haven from hunters. These winter residents include flamingos, pelicans, swans, herons, egrets, sandpipers, and a variety of ducks and geese. Common inland birds are the pheasant, the rock partridge, and bustards.

The Caspian Sea and the Kura River support abundant fish life, but the Caspian has suffered severe environmental damage, largely from the oil-extracting practices in place under Soviet rule. Pollution, combined with overfishing, has greatly reduced the catch of sturgeons—fish prized for producing roe that is made into the world's best caviar. Other fish common to the Kura and the Caspian are herring, perch, and pike.

In 2019, about a dozen zoo-bred bison such as this wisent were released into Azerbaijan's Shahdag National Park to reintroduce this animal that went extinct in the wild in the 1920s.

CITIES

There are 77 cities in Azerbaijan, along with 257 towns and 4,620 villages.

BAKU The country's capital city, Baku, is on the southern shore of the Absheron Peninsula, the slightly curved, pointed extension of land that reaches about 37 miles (60 km) east into the Caspian Sea. The city overlooks the Bay of Baku, a natural harbor on the underside of the peninsula's curve. Sitting at a depth of 92 feet (28 m) below sea level, Baku has the distinction of being the lowest-lying capital in the world. About one-quarter of Azerbaijan's population live in this metropolitan district.

Baku is an active port city, as well as the scientific, cultural, industrial, and business center of Azerbaijan. With its many futuristic and spectacular skyscrapers and other architecturally impressive buildings, its shopping malls, and its popular museums, theaters, sports venues, parks, and nightspots, Baku attracts many tourists.

This aerial view shows how Baku curves around Baku Bay of the Caspian Sea.

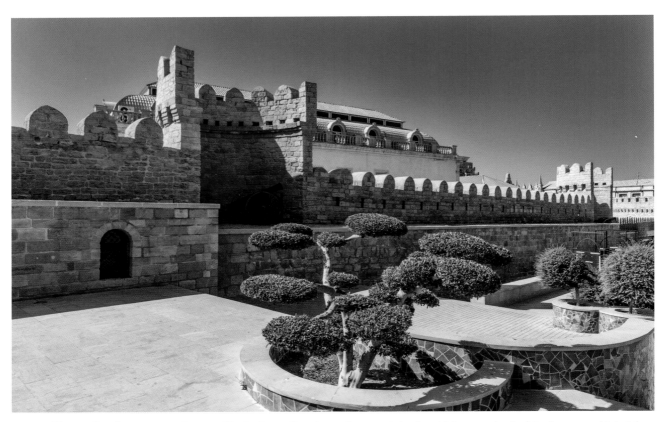

The walls of Baku's Old Town are among the architectural highlights of the city.

The Walled City of Baku, along with the Shirvanshahs' Palace and Maiden Tower, is a UNESCO World Heritage Site. The site has been inhabited since prehistoric times, and it shows the influences of many ancient cultures. Its defensive walls, built in the 12th century, enclose an inner city of architectural treasures. The Maiden Tower is a national symbol of Azerbaijan and the source of numerous legends and mysteries. The 15th-century Palace of the Shirvanshahs, also located in the walled city, is another of the country's architectural symbols.

SUMQAYIT   Located on the Caspian Sea on the northern side of the Absheron Peninsula, this city is about 19 miles (31 km) from Baku and has a population of about 341,200 people. (It's an extension of the Baku metropolitan area.) The city has an unfortunate reputation for severe pollution, stemming from its heavy industrialization during the Soviet years.

GANJA   This city in northwestern Azerbaijan is either the second- or third-largest city in the country, depending on the source. It has about 332,600 residents, many of whom are ethnic Azerbaijanis from Armenia. There are also thousands who fled the region of Nagorno-Karabkh. The city has changed names several times. Under Russian occupation in the 19th to 20th centuries, it was called Elisabethpol, and in 1935, under the Soviets, its name was changed to Kirovabad. In 1989, it regained its original name of Ganja. Today, it is one of the most famous tourist destinations in Azerbaijan, with historic buildings and cultural, shopping, recreational, and natural attractions.

INTERNET LINKS

https://www.azconsulatela.org/Azerbaijan/Land-and-Nature/Geography
A short overview on Azerbaijan's geography includes links to related topics.

https://www.economist.com/the-economist-explains/2018/08/16/is-the-caspian-a-sea-or-a-lake
An article in *The Economist* discusses the political ramifications of how the Caspian is classified.

https://theculturetrip.com/europe/azerbaijan/articles/lake-goygol-azerbaijans-ethereal-landscape
Lake Goygol is just one of several places highlighted in this travel site's Azerbaijan section.

https://www.usgs.gov/center-news/volcano-watch-heres-dirty-truth-about-mud-volcanoes
A short article explains the science behind mud volcanoes.

https://whc.unesco.org/en/statesparties/az
This is the World Heritage page for sites in Azerbaijan.

HISTORY

Ancient rock carvings, or petroglyphs, in Gobustan
National Park show figures of people with a boat.

THE FIRST HUMAN SETTLEMENTS IN what is now Azerbaijan date back to the Stone Age, more than 12,000 years ago. Hundreds of cave dwellings have been excavated throughout the country. The most impressive evidence of Stone Age life consists of more than 6,000 engravings, called petroglyphs, found on cave walls in Gobustan, near the coast of the Caspian Sea.

Azerbaijan's geographical location has had a powerful influence on its history. Situated in the Caucasus region between the Caspian and Black Seas, Azerbaijan has long been a vital crossroads between Asia and Europe. Great empires have collided there, and some of history's most famous conquerors have fought for the land, including Cyrus the Great, Pompey, Alexander the Great, Timur, and Genghis Khan.

CONQUEST AND CHANGE

During the fourth century CE, missionaries from Armenia spread Christianity into the area known as Caucasian Albania (including today's Azerbaijan), and a large portion of the population was converted. Over the next 300 or 400 years, dozens of Christian churches were built. Ruins of these ancient structures still dot the landscape.

2

Rarely has Azerbaijan had the peace and stability needed to build a strong independent state. Instead, through most of its history, it has been a province ruled by Persia, Russia, or some other powerful empire.

Christianity did not dominate permanently, however. In 642 CE, Arab Muslim armies swept into Caucasian Albania. The land became part of the vast Islamic empire, which sprawled from Asia through the Middle East and into North Africa. Islam soon dominated Caucasian Albania, which became a province within the empire.

In the 11th century, another Islamic power gained control. These new invaders were from Turkish tribes who were part of the Seljuk dynasty. The conquest led to a blending of peoples, cultures, and languages. The original population, largely descended from Persians, began to merge with the Turks, and the Persian language was replaced by a Turkic dialect that slowly evolved into modern Azeri, the language of Azerbaijan.

In 1236, the Mongol warriors of Genghis Khan's powerful empire in the East conquered what is today called Azerbaijan and remained in control until 1498. Around 1500, a new Persian kingdom was formed under the Safavid dynasty, which had its capital at Tabriz (in today's northwestern Iran). The new rulers established the Shia (or Shiite) branch of Islam as the official religion, and this dominance continues today.

During the reign of the Safavids, Azerbaijan was frequently a battleground in a power struggle between Persia and Russia. Safavid rule ended in 1722, and northern Azerbaijan splintered into several principalities, or khanates (areas governed by a khan, or ruler). These divisions made it easier for Russia to move in and seize power. The Persians fought back in two Russo-Persian wars: in 1804 to 1813 and 1826 to 1828.

Russia's victories gave it control over most of northern Azerbaijan, and the Aras River became the region's permanent dividing line. This advance made Russia the first European nation to move into the Middle East. About half of the Azerbaijani people remained south of the Aras within Persia in what would become known as the Azerbaijan region of Iran.

Under Russian rule, northern Azerbaijan began a period of development far different from what happened on the Persian side of the Aras River. When oil was discovered in the area around Baku, the modern industrial age arrived in the nation almost overnight. Baku became the center of a fantastic oil boom. Workers and oil companies swarmed into the area, creating a multiethnic boomtown in which Azerbaijanis made up less than half the population.

By 1900, Azerbaijan was producing half the world's oil, and the oil refining industry had its beginnings there. However, the great boom did not last. As new sources of oil were found in other parts of Russia and the world, less and less development money was spent in Azerbaijan. Since no manufacturing industries had been set up, hundreds of workers joined the ranks of the unemployed, and the mansions of the oil barons were abandoned.

THE SOVIET UNION

In 1917, a revolution in Russia brought the empire to an end. Then, the provisional democratic government was overthrown by the Bolshevik wing of the Communist Party. Russia became the Soviet Union. In Azerbaijan, a small group of professionals known as the intelligentsia joined with workers in Baku to form a democratic government. However, in April 1920, the Soviet Union's Red Army invaded and quickly ended Azerbaijan's brief period as an independent state.

This engraving from an 1886 edition of *The Illustrated London News* shows a "gusher" spouting oil before being brought under control in a Baku oil field.

For a few years starting in 1922, the three regions of Transcaucasia—Azerbaijan, Armenia, and Georgia—were joined in a loose federation called the Transcaucasian Soviet Federated Socialist Republic (TSFSR). This attempt to create regional unity did not bring an end to the seething ethnic conflict that gripped the small mountainous area on the Azerbaijan-Armenia border called Nagorno-Karabakh. The conflict, which pitted Armenian Christians against Muslim Azerbaijanis, grew bitter and sometimes violent during various periods in the 20th and 21st centuries.

Under Soviet rule, the Azerbaijani members of the intelligentsia were given special treatment when it came to filling government jobs. With the support of Soviet communists, these leaders tried to create a secular state—a society in which organized religion would have no influence. The government closed mosques, outlawed religious education, and imprisoned dozens of Muslim clerics.

This vicious campaign practically destroyed the institution of Islam in Azerbaijan, but the religion remained central to people's personal lives. The majority of Azerbaijanis continued to live according to the traditions, beliefs, and prohibitions of Islam.

In the 1930s, Azerbaijan experienced a new wave of violence as Joseph Stalin, dictator of the Soviet Union, began a systematic campaign to destroy all opposition to his rule. He found a useful henchman in Mir Jafar Baghirov, first secretary of the Communist Party of Azerbaijan. First the intelligentsia was purged of potential enemies, then the party itself was purged. More than 100,000 Azerbaijanis (sometimes called Azeris) were executed or sent to concentration camps in the Soviet Union. In 1936, the attempt to create a unified Transcaucasian republic ended. The Azerbaijani Soviet Socialist Republic became a separate republic within the Soviet Union.

WORLD WAR II AND AFTER

During World War II (1939–1945), Germany was eager to reach the oil fields of the Soviet Union and the Middle East. In June 1941, German armies invaded the Soviet Union and reached the Greater Caucasus Mountains a year later. The Soviet Red Army, aided by Azerbaijani and Armenian troops, managed to keep the Germans from crossing into Azerbaijan.

Another wartime event led to the possibility that Iranian Azerbaijan might be united with the Republic of Azerbaijan. In mid-1941, Soviet forces occupied Iranian Azerbaijan, which led to a revival of unification ideas, known as the Pan-Azerbaijani movement. Soviet leaders even supported an independent Azerbaijani people's government at Tabriz. When the war ended, however, the Western Allies, led by the United States and Great Britain, insisted that the Russians withdraw.

The brutality of Stalin's rule ended with Stalin's death and the leadership of Nikita Khrushchev (1953–1964). During what was called the Khrushchev Thaw, Soviet rule of Azerbaijan became more relaxed. Censorship of the press was eased, as was control of scholarship and literature.

Although the post-Stalin era meant a lessening of dictatorial controls, Azerbaijan suffered a period of economic stagnation beginning in the 1960s. The

Soviet government failed to invest any money in the declining Baku oil fields. Outdated equipment and a lack of environmental concern were transforming the western Caspian Sea into an environmental nightmare. During the same period, the Soviets decided to make the city of Sumqayit the capital of a new petrochemical industry. The country's third-largest city produced its own ecological horror as chemicals poisoned the air, water, and land.

ETHNIC CONFLICT

By the late 1980s, the seemingly indestructible Soviet Union had begun to crumble. One after another, the former Communist satellite states of central and eastern Europe claimed their independence. As with the rest of the Soviet republics, Azerbaijan declared its independence. This happened on August 30, 1991. The last of the Azerbaijani Communist Party leaders, Ayaz N. Mutalibov, was elected president of the new republic.

This memorial in Baku honors Soviet soldiers who died defending the city during World War II.

Hopes for a new age of independence were overshadowed, however, by the Azeri-Armenian conflict playing out along the border between the two republics. Soviet power had kept the dispute in check, but after the collapse of the Soviet Union, warfare erupted in Nagorno-Karabakh. Armenian troops, most of them trained in the Soviet army, quickly gained the upper hand. President Mutalibov was reluctant to increase the Azerbaijani army's presence in the region for fear that he would not be able to control his forces. In 1992, when Armenian troops massacred Azerbaijani civilians at Xocali, Mutalibov was removed. A new president, Abulfaz Elchibey, replaced him in June 1992.

Elchibey also failed to stop the bloodshed in Nagorno-Karabakh. By early 1993, Armenia had control of nearly 20 percent of Azerbaijan's territory. The Azerbaijani military rebelled in June 1993, forcing Elchibey to flee. The former president hid in his hometown and refused to resign.

The rebellion provided the opportunity for Heydar Aliyev, chairman of the parliament, to seize power. Aliyev, a former member of the Soviet KGB (secret police), had been unable to run in the presidential election because he was older than the age limit of 65. From his headquarters in Naxcivan, he built a loyal following and, while Elchibey was in hiding, went to Baku, where he declared himself interim president. An election was held in October 1993, and Aliyev won an overwhelming victory.

With his power secure, Aliyev signed a cease-fire with Armenia and Nagorno-Karabakh in 1994. The arrangement left 13 percent of Azerbaijani land under Armenian control, and 800,000 Azeris became refugees in what had been their own country. Later in 1994, Aliyev concluded what was called the contract of the century—an oil contract worth $7.4 billion from a consortium of several oil companies to develop the Caspian Sea oil and gas reserves and share the proceeds with the state oil company.

Azerbaijani children, refugees from the Nagorno-Karabakh region, attend an improvised school surrounded by abandoned oil derricks in 1997. Homeless families from the war-torn area were forced to live in poverty on vacated, polluted sections of old oil fields in Baku.

THE WAR FOR NAGORNO-KARABAKH

Nagorno-Karabakh, which its people now call the Republic of Artsakh, takes up the southwestern quadrant of Azerbaijan. It is a place of rugged beauty—heavily forested mountains, steep-sided valleys, and picturesque farms and pastures. Today, the region is home to about 145,000 people, almost entirely ethnic Armenians. Its capital is Stepanakert, with a population of around 55,000.

In 1989, the largely Armenian Christian population voted for independence from Azerbaijan. Under Soviet rule, a somewhat smaller Nagorno-Karabakh had been an autonomous (self-governing) oblast (province). For the next five years, the region was the scene of bitter warfare as the outnumbered residents tried to withstand constant bombardment by Azeribaijani and Russian forces. When the Soviet Union collapsed, the war changed dramatically—Armenian troops

Once a city of 28,000 people, **Agdam** is now a ghost town of bombed-out ruins in **Nagorno-Karabakh**.

aided the Karabakhian commandos and forced the Azerbaijani army to retreat.

An estimated 500,000 Azerbaijani Muslims were forced to flee. Since the cease-fire was established in 1994, Nagorno-Karabakh has struggled to rebuild, and the task seems overwhelming. Roughly 30,000 citizens were killed in the war and, in addition to widespread damage, the region was left with hundreds of thousands of hidden land mines. International organizations have tried to negotiate a permanent settlement, but so far, no solution has been found. In fact, in 2020, tensions began reigniting once again, resulting in violence and death.

THE 21ST CENTURY

Toward the end of his life, the ailing Heydar Aliyev pushed to have his son succeed him in office. Heydar Aliyev died in December 2003, and his son Ilham became president in spite of protests. He was reelected to a fourth term in 2018 with 86 percent of the votes in an election that Western observers found problematic. He appointed his wife, Mehriban, as the first vice president, and some think he is preparing his son to succeed him.

Azerbaijan President Ilham Aliyev (*center*) attends a Victory Day event in Baku on May 9, 2019.

Under Ilham Aliyev, the country has become wealthier and more modern. His reforms have driven economic growth and lifted living standards for many citizens, which, of course, helped increase his popularity. He also established strong relationships with many countries, especially in regards to expanding his nation's oil industry.

But many international observers are uneasy about Aliyev's leadership. He's now into his fourth term as president, and it seems clear that he intends to be the country's president for a very long time to come—and if not him, then a member of his family. Over the course of his rule, he has become increasingly intolerant of dissent, especially in the media. Aliyev points to this nation's stability in the face of rising tensions in many other countries as proof that his firm hand, if not iron fist, is the stabilizing factor.

INTERNET LINKS

https://www.bbc.com/news/world-europe-17047328
BBC News has a helpful timeline of key events in modern Azerbaijan.

https://blogs.kent.ac.uk/carc/2018/04/15/the-nagorno-karabakh-conflict
This page uses maps and graphics to explain the Nagorno-Karabakh conflict.

https://www.britannica.com/place/Azerbaijan
Encyclopedia Britannica provides a thorough overview of the country's history.

https://neweasterneurope.eu/2019/08/21/is-a-new-war-in-karabakh-inevitable
This article examines the mounting tensions between Azerbaijan and Armenia.

GOVERNMENT

ALİ MƏHKƏMƏ

The flag of Azerbaijan flies over the
Supreme Court building in Baku.

3

THE REPUBLIC OF AZERBAIJAN IS A presidential republic. According to *The World Factbook,* published by the U.S. Central Intelligence Agency (CIA), that means the following: "Presidential—a system of government where the executive branch exists separately from a legislature (to which it is generally not accountable)"; and "Republic—a representative democracy in which the people's elected deputies (representatives), not the people themselves, vote on legislation."

Azerbaijan began its existence as an independent nation on August 30, 1991, with Ayaz Mutalibov, former first secretary of the Azerbaijani Communist Party, becoming the country's first president. However, the government's first years were unstable. The country had to shake off the concept of government it had endured for nearly 70 years as a communist entity within the enormous Union of Soviet Socialist Republics (USSR), or Soviet Union. (A *soviet* was originally a communist workers' council; and ultimately, a communist governmental body.)

According to the CIA *World Factbook*, communism is "a system of government in which the state plans and controls the economy and a single—often authoritarian—party holds power; state controls are

In 2017, the Republic of Artsakh (Nagorno-Karabkh) became a presidential democracy following a constitutional referendum. Since 2020, the president has been Arayik Harutyunyan. The president is directly elected for a maximum of two consecutive five-year terms. The National Assembly is a unicameral legislature, with 33 members who are elected for five-year terms.

imposed with the elimination of private ownership of property or capital while claiming to make progress toward a higher social order in which all goods are equally shared by the people (for example, a classless society)."

SOVIET RULE

From the 1920s to 1991, Azerbaijan was one of the 15 republics that made up the Soviet Union. A new constitution for the republic, approved in 1937, declared that Azerbaijan was a sovereign state and equal to all other Soviet republics. In reality, however, the government of Azerbaijan had no control over foreign affairs, military matters, or long-range economic planning. There was even little self-government in terms of domestic politics, and all questions involving ideology and culture were decided in Moscow, the seat of government power in Russia.

Even Azerbaijan's government structure was copied from that of the Soviet Union. The supreme soviet was the legislature, with members chosen from a slate of candidates approved by the Communist Party. The highest executive and administrative body was the council of ministers. The judiciary consisted of a supreme court and a lower court.

Like all the Soviet republics, Azerbaijan's role was to advance the welfare of the entire Soviet Union. Agriculture was promoted, for example, so that planners in Moscow could direct a percentage of all agricultural products to the parts of the USSR where they were most needed. Similarly, large sums were invested in the Baku oil fields, but when oil resources in other parts of the Soviet Union seemed more profitable, the Baku region was largely ignored. Such projects of industrialization were routinely developed in the Soviet years with no regard for the environment. This has left a disastrous legacy of pollution in the Baku region.

INDEPENDENCE AND ETHNIC WARFARE

As soon as the Soviet Union began its collapse in the late 1980s, political leaders in Azerbaijan were ready. However, Ayaz Mutalibov, the new republic's first president, was not prepared to deal with the deep-seated ethnic conflict between the Azerbaijanis and the Armenians.

One advantage of the years of stern Soviet rule was that it kept those ethnic and religious rivalries under control. In the spring of 1992, Mutalibov's failure to handle the problem led to his removal. The opposition Popular Front Party (PFP) assumed power and dissolved the largely communist Supreme Soviet, transferring authority to a 50-member national council, the upper house of the legislature.

A new president, PFP leader Abulfez Elchibey, also failed to resolve the bloody warfare in the territory of Nagorno-Karabakh. Many Azerbaijanis charged his administration with corruption and incompetence. In June 1993, an anti-government uprising in the city of Ganja forced Elchibey to flee. As armed rebels advanced on Baku, the capital, the national council gave presidential powers to its new speaker, Heydar Aliyev. As president, Aliyev exercised enormous power. Since 2003, his son and successor, Ilham Aliyev, has amassed far more.

THE CONSTITUTION

The nation's present constitution was adopted on November 12, 1995, by popular referendum. November 12 is now celebrated as Constitution Day. This is the country's first constitution as an independent state; prior constitutions were in accordance with the constitution of the Soviet Union. Since its adoption, the constitution has been amended several times, with numerous additions and changes. In 2002, 31 amendments were made; in 2009, 41 amendments were made; and in 2016, 23 articles were amended, and 6 new articles were added.

The document declares that "the Azerbaijan State is a democratic, law-governed, secular, unitary republic." It guarantees a democratic system, in which "the Azerbaijan people are the sole source of State power." Freedoms, rights, and responsibilities are spelled out, with equal rights afforded to all, regardless of "race, ethnicity, religion, sex, origin, property status, social position, convictions, political party, trade union organization, and social unity affiliation."

Heydar Aliyev (1923–2003) first rose to power in the Azerbaijani Communist Party, then became part of the Soviet KGB, a post in which he revealed his ruthless side during the 1960s. He was the first Azerbaijani to serve as a member of the Politburo, the supreme policy-making authority of the Soviet Union. In the spirit of greater freedom that followed the end of the Cold War, Soviet premier Mikhail Gorbachev had him removed following charges of corruption.

For a few years, Aliyev almost disappeared, but the instability that developed following independence gave him a new opportunity. He reinvented himself as a strong leader committed to developing Azerbaijan's oil wealth. From 1993 onward, Aliyev ruled the republic with an iron fist. Nevertheless, he brought stability to the country, instituted important land reforms, and established balanced relationships with other nations and international organizations. He also rebuilt his country's oil sector by attracting foreign investment.

Opponents could not prevent him from grooming his son, Ilham, as his successor. Although Ilham had the reputation of being a playboy and a gambler, he became vice chairman of the state oil company, as well as the country's representative to the Council of Europe and president of the Azerbaijani Olympic committee. The younger Aliyev is also well-educated; he has a doctorate in history.

In October 2003, as Heydar was in grave health, he appointed Ilham to take over the presidency. Ilham went on to win the subsequent presidential election with nearly 77 percent of the vote. He then won the 2008 election with 87 percent of the vote. At that point, a constitutional amendment did away with term limits for the presidency, paving the way for Aliyev to stay in power. He won the 2013 and 2018 elections by equally high margins. Although Aliyev supposedly enjoys great popularity in the country, all of the elections were deemed by international observers to be tainted.

In 2017, Aliyev appointed his wife, Mehriban Aliyeva, shown here with him, as "first vice president." Prior to that, the country had no vice presidents. The move was enabled by a group of constitutional amendments that also extended the presidential term from five to seven years and eliminated any age limit for the president. These moves further established an ongoing political dynasty in Azerbaijan.

Other rights include the right to social security, to live in a healthy environment, to health protection, and to education. Citizens also enjoy freedom of religion, freedom of movement and assembly, and freedom of speech, conscience, and thought. Freedom of the press is also supposed to protected: "The freedom of mass media is guaranteed. State censorship of mass media, including print media, is forbidden." Nevertheless, the Aliyev regime has faced strong international criticism for suppressing dissent and opposition media.

The principal obligations of citizens, according to the constitution, include obeying the laws, paying taxes, demonstrating loyalty and allegiance to the homeland, serving in the defense of the homeland, and showing respect for state symbols.

The Government House of Azerbaijan glows in the sunshine in Baku. Built between 1936 and 1955, it was renovated in the early 2000s. The large building houses several state ministries.

THE EXECUTIVE BRANCH

THE PRESIDENT is the head of state and the head of the executive branch. He or she is directly elected by the people in an absolute majority vote and serves for seven-year terms with no term limit. The last election was in 2018, and the next is to be held in 2025. The first vice president is appointed by the president; there are also additional vice presidents as determined by the president. The president appoints all cabinet-level government administrators and heads of local executive bodies.

THE PRIME MINISTER is the head of government. He or she is nominated by the president and confirmed by the National Assembly. The prime minister's power is secondary to the president's, and the president may revoke any act of the government.

The preamble to the constitution of Azerbaijan states that its mission is "to provide a democratic system." Any country may call itself a democracy, but how well does the description fit the reality? In some cases, there's quite a wide gap between the high-minded words in a nation's constitution and the actuality. It all depends on how well a government functions to protect democratic principles.

Several international organizations watch closely to evaluate how well the world's governments are doing on that score.

Freedom House is a U.S.-based independent watchdog organization that conducts research on democracy, political freedom, and human rights. In its annual Freedom in the World report, it ranks nations on such matters and assigns a finding of "Free," "Partly Free," or "Not Free."

In its 2019 report, it took a decidedly dim view of freedom in Azerbaijan, ranking it "Not Free" with an aggregate score of 10 out of 100. For comparison, the United States ranked 86, earning the rank of "Free." Finland, Norway, and Sweden all earned a perfect score of 100; with Syria coming in last with a "Not Free" score of 0.

The report pointed to the authoritarian regime of President Ilham Aliyev, who has been in power since 2003 (succeeding his father) and who appointed his wife as vice president in 2017. The family appears to be set to remain in power indefinitely. The report also points to fraudulent elections, rampant corruption, intimidation and imprisonment of journalists, and extreme restrictions on civil liberties.

THE LEGISLATIVE BRANCH

The parliament, or National Assembly, is a unicameral (one-house) body called the Milli Majlis (or Mejlis). It consists of 125 members who are directly elected and who serve five-year terms. Religious figures are not allowed to serve in this capacity. The last parliamentary election was in 2020, with the next one scheduled for 2025. In 2020, the members included 104 men and 21 women.

THE JUDICIAL SYSTEM

The highest courts are the Supreme Court and the Constitutional Court. The Supreme Court is the court of highest, or last, appeal. It includes a chairman, a vice chairman, and 23 judges organized into various chambers—civil, economic affairs, criminal, and rights violations. The Constitutional Court determines the constitutionality of laws; it is made up of nine judges. All of these judges are appointed by or nominated by the president. Supreme Court judges serve for 10 years; Constitutional Court judges serve for 15 years.

Lower courts include the courts of appeal as well as district and municipal courts. Cases are first tried at the district level. The judgment can be appealed at one of six courts of appeal. A final appeal may be heard at the Supreme Court level, and that is the final verdict.

INTERNET LINKS

https://www.cia.gov/library/publications/the-world-factbook/geos/aj.html
The World Factbook has up-to-date information about the government of Azerbaijan.

https://www.constituteproject.org/constitution/Azerbaijan_2016.pdf?lang=en
This site provides the content of Azerbaijan's constitution in English.

ECONOMY

The Azerbaijani manat, the country's currency, is shown here in banknotes. The 200-manat bill (in blue) features the Heydar Aliyev Center in Baku. It was issued in 2018 to commemorate former President Heydar Aliyev's 95th birthday.

4

I N THE EARLY YEARS OF independence, Azerbaijan had its work cut out for it in trying to repair and recharge its economy. Its experience as a Soviet republic had taken its toll. In the late 1980s, communism collapsed as a viable economic model, and with it, the Soviet Union. Throughout Eastern Europe and Western Asia, former communist economies such as Azerbaijan's had to switch to a whole new structure. The transition took time.

State ownership of land and businesses had to be transferred to private ownership, a daunting task. By 2004, most agricultural land was in private hands. The same was true of small and medium-sized businesses. However, the government has continued to play a major role in the economy, especially in the control of major enterprises such as the oil industry and other energy sources.

During the years of Soviet control, there was serious mismanagement of Azerbaijan's resources. Planners in Moscow did not hesitate to use outdated equipment and methods in the rush to exploit the Baku oil fields. The result is a legacy of environmental pollution that will take years to repair. Soviet planners followed much the same methods in establishing

One of the early investors in the Baku oil fields in the 1890s was Alfred Nobel, the Swedish-born inventor of dynamite and other explosives. Nobel used the fortune he acquired from these investments to establish the Nobel Prizes, the world's highest honors given in specific areas of the social and natural sciences as well as for literature and the promotion of peace.

a major petrochemical industry at Sumqayit, Azerbaijan's third-largest city, also located on the Absheron Peninsula. Yet another ecological disaster ensued.

OIL AND OTHER NATURAL RESOURCES

Petroleum became one of the world's most important energy resources in the late 1800s, and Azerbaijan was one of the pioneers in its development. The underground oil reserves around Baku on the Absheron Peninsula were so close to the surface in some places that they bubbled up on their own. Search teams quickly found that there was even more oil—and natural gas—beneath the Caspian Sea. Foreign companies and workers rushed to join the Azerbaijani efforts and, by 1900, the Baku fields were producing roughly half the world's oil. The technology for refining the oil was also first developed in Baku. The city is still home to the many mansions built during the great oil boom.

After 1920, under Soviet rule, Azerbaijan's oil production gradually declined, although it still remained important in the late 1900s. After Azerbaijan declared

Oil pumps and rigs fill a field by the Caspian Sea near Baku.

Gross domestic product (GDP) is a measure of a country's total production. The number reflects the total value of goods and services produced over one year. Economists use it to determine whether a country's economy is growing or contracting. Growth is good, while a falling GDP means trouble. Dividing the GDP by the number of people in the country determines the GDP per capita (per person). This number provides an indication of a country's average standard of living—the higher the better.

In 2017, the GDP per capita (adjusted to purchasing power parity) in Azerbaijan was approximately $17,500. The 2017 figure is considered medium, and it ranked Azerbaijan at 101st out of 228 countries listed by the CIA World Factbook. For comparison, the United States that year was number 19, with a GDP per capita of $59,500. Azerbaijan's neighbor Armenia scored much lower at 142, with $9,500; neighbor Georgia was not much better at number 138 with $10,700. Azerbaijan's neighbor to the south, Iran, came in at number 89 that year, with a GDP per capita of $20,100.

its independence from the crumbling Soviet empire in 1991, the new republic's oil production suffered for several years, partly because of the antiquated Soviet equipment and also because of the ethnic conflicts between Christian Armenians and Muslim Azerbaijanis.

The deal that President Heydar Aliyev arranged in 1994 to 1995 started Azerbaijan on the path to regain its position as one of the world's leading oil producers. Until a global decline in oil prices in 2014—resulting from decreasing demand and other factors—Azerbaijan's high economic growth was mostly based on rising energy exports.

Today, oil remains the basis of Azerbaijan's economy, but efforts to boost Azerbaijan's gas production are underway. The completion of the important Southern Gas Corridor (SGC) pipelines between Azerbaijan and Europe is expected to open up another source of revenue from gas exports. The gas pipelines draw largely from the Shah Deniz gas field in the South Caspian Sea, the largest natural gas field in Azerbaijan.

The country also has rich supplies of other natural resources, including lead, zinc, iron, and copper ores, as well as building materials such as limestone and marble.

AGRICULTURE

Azerbaijan imports more food than it exports. Nevertheless, agriculture plays an important role in its economy. Plentiful water for irrigation and different climatic zones combine to make a wide variety of crops possible, from those that thrive in cold winters and mild summers to crops such as tea and citrus fruit that need subtropical conditions. About 40 percent of the nation's landmass is suitable for agriculture, and more than half of that potential farmland is currently under cultivation.

In 2017, agriculture accounted for 6.1 percent of the GDP, but it employed 37 percent of the labor force. The government has instituted reforms aimed at increasing crop production to make this sector more profitable. Boosting

Farmers harvest cotton in the Neftchala District in the south of Azerbaijan.

various agricultural sectors will also help to diversify the nation's economy, buffering it from the ups and downs of the world oil and energy market.

Grain is the republic's leading crop, with wheat being the most abundant grain and barley coming in second. Wheat contributes to more than 50 percent of the daily intake of calories in the Azerbaijani diet. Despite its status as the country's largest crop, more wheat needs to be imported as well.

Grapes have become increasingly important. Most of that crop is used to make wine—one of Azerbaijan's major exports. Other crops include vegetables, including eggplants; fruits such as pomegranates and figs; and nuts such as walnuts and hazelnuts. Tea and citrus fruits are grown in the south. Also, areas around the towns of Sheki, Zagatala, and Goychay have long been involved in the breeding of silkworms.

FISHERIES

Herring, pike, and perch are fished from the Kura and other rivers, and trout are found in mountain streams. However, it is the Caspian Sea that is the source of one of Azerbaijan's most treasured products.

That body of water has long been world famous as a major source of caviar, which is still a valuable export. The roe (fish eggs) is salted in order to bring out the flavor, as well as to preserve it. Beluga caviar, which comes from a particular species of sturgeon, is considered a great delicacy and ranks as one of the world's most expensive foods.

Over the past century, sturgeon fishing has declined steadily, in part because of the Caspian Sea's pollution from oil, sewage, and chemicals. The results of overfishing are also a major reason for the decline.

TRANSPORTATION

Since there are few navigable rivers in Azerbaijan, most freight is carried by railroad and truck. The Absheron region, including Baku and Sumqayit, is the most urbanized and industrialized part of Azerbaijan. Several highways link this region to all parts of the republic as well as to neighboring countries such

Tourism has been a rapidly growing sector of Azerbaijan's economy. In 2019, a record-setting 3.17 million tourists arrived there from 191 countries, in a trend that has been increasing annually through much of the 21st century. The largest number of visitors came from South Asian and Central Asian countries, as well as from Russia. About 224,000 visitors came from Europe, a 14.7 percent increase over the previous year.

Emphasizing its motto as "Land of Fire," Azerbaijan is working to build up its tourism industry as a way of lessening its reliance on the oil industry. The country's main attraction is Baku, with its UNESCO-listed Old City and the rest of the city's impressive new architecture. The natural fires of Azerbaijan, which lend the place its nickname, lure tourists to Yanar Dag ("Fire Mountain") just outside Baku, where a nearly continuous natural fire burns on a hillside. The Gobustan National Park is another attraction, featuring mud volcanoes, prehistoric rock art, extraordinary landscapes, and a museum. Health spas offer another enticement to global travelers, as do resorts on the Caspian or in the Caucasus Mountains.

Visitors view the burning mountain of Yanar Dag in September 2019.

as Iran, Turkey, Georgia, and Russia. Nearly 2,000 miles (3,219 km) of railways also carry freight from the peninsula throughout the country. In October 2017, the long-awaited Baku-Tbilisi-Kars railway, stretching from the Azerbaijani capital to Kars in northeastern Turkey, began limited service.

Baku is also a major port on the Caspian Sea. Bulk freight items such as grain, timber, and oil are shipped to Asia, Russia, and Iran. There are also ferry services and passenger lines.

In addition, Baku has air service to many cities in Europe and Asia. Azerbaijan Airlines is the flag carrier for the country and operates out of Heydar Aliyev International Airport in Baku, the largest of six international airports in the country.

INTERNET LINKS

https://www.cnn.com/travel/article/yanar-dag-azerbaijan-land-of-fire/index.html
This article explores the "eternal flame" of Yanar Dag.

https://en.president.az/articles/35601
The text of a 2019 speech by President Ilham Aliyev reports on his nation's economic growth.

https://www.heritage.org/index/country/azerbaijan
The Index of Economic Freedom looks at the country's business climate.

http://Naxcivan.preslib.az/en_e1.html
This page provides an overview of the Naxcivan Autonomous Republic's economy.

https://www.worldbank.org/en/country/azerbaijan
The World Bank offers an overview of Azerbaijan's economy.

ENVIRONMENT

Household waste pollutes the environment in Salyan, Azerbaijan.

5

T HE ABSHERON PENINSULA AND THE surrounding Caspian Sea are among the most ecologically devastated areas in the world. The region's soil is polluted from decades of oil spills, from the use of DDT pesticide, and from toxic defoliants used in the production of cotton. Surface and underground water are polluted by untreated municipal and industrial wastewater and agricultural runoff. Air pollution has been caused by industrial emissions from the oil and gas industries, power plants, and vehicular traffic.

THE SOVIET LEGACY

Throughout the 20th century, Soviet planners were intent on taking as much of the republic's oil—and other natural resources—as quickly and as cheaply as possible. Primitive drilling platforms were built off Baku in the Caspian, using antiquated equipment and techniques. The new burst of activity led to more accidents and increased damage to the sea and land. The damage caused by the Soviet Union's reckless exploitation of

In the 2018 Environmental Performance Index, Azerbaijan ranked 59th of 180 countries in an overall assessment of its environment. That's not too bad. However, certain areas stand out as being particularly in need of attention. In air quality, for example, it ranked number 153, and in water and sanitation, it ranked 94th. While these rankings mean Azerbaijan is not the worst country in the world for these concerns, there is room for improvement.

the republic's oil resources made the Absheron Peninsula and its Caspian Sea shoreline one of the most polluted areas in the world.

In the 1950s, as oil production declined, Soviet planners shifted their focus to Sumqayit, a city on the northern coast of the peninsula. At its peak, Sumqayit was a booming industrial town, creating a new wave of prosperity but at an enormous cost. Scores of factory chimneys spewed ugly brown and yellow clouds, producing a permanent unhealthy haze. In addition to oil slicks and polluted air and water, there were growing reports of people, especially children, contracting fatal diseases and an alarming increase in birth defects.

With the demise of the Soviet Union, the newly independent republic of Azerbaijan was left to clean up the wreckage. The task was delayed by the war in Nagorno-Karabakh, by the political upheaval that followed, and by a lack of funds. Now that the economy is doing better, cleanup efforts are underway, and the air and water have improved.

Oily pollution flows from pumps on the shore in Baku. Much of the infrastructure in these oil fields is old and poorly maintained by SOCAR, the state oil company.

A unique artifact from the days of Soviet oil production is the world's first offshore oil rig. Built on massive stilts, rocks, and seven sunken ships, the complex is called Neft Dashlari ("Oil Rocks"). More than an oil platform, it's a small floating city, nicknamed "Stalin's Atlantis" after the Soviet dictator Joseph Stalin.

It once had apartments for 5,000 workers as well as a bakery, a school, and a movie theater. Located around 34 miles (55 km) off the tip of the Absheron Peninsula in the Caspian Sea, the rig had around 2,000 drilling platforms joined by an intricate network of roads and low-lying bridges extending approximately 18 miles (29 km) across the sea.

By the later part of the 20th century, the massive structure began to fall into disrepair. The roadways rusted and fell into the sea. Production slowed considerably but did continue, even though the equipment was antiquated. Today, the floating city is shrouded in secret; it doesn't even appear on Google Maps.

Oil Rocks celebrated its 60th anniversary in 2009. At that time, the State Oil Company of Azerbaijan Republic (SOCAR) said the unit had extracted around 170 million tons (154 million metric tons) of oil from the Caspian over its lifetime. The company claimed there were still another 30 million tons (27 million metric tons) under the sea, but by then, the oil city was deteriorating badly. Since that time, more information about the place has become unavailable.

RESTORING FARMLAND

Another environmental problem Azerbaijan inherited from Soviet rule is serious land pollution. In the effort to increase agricultural production on government-controlled farmland, toxic defoliants were used to clear forests for

crops, and DDT was used long after it had been discontinued in other countries. These toxic substances not only poisoned the soil but also leached into the groundwater, polluting streams, ponds, and lakes.

Safer farming methods are now in place, and several pesticides and herbicides have been banned. So far, however, few funds have been allocated for major cleanup and prevention programs. A number of international agencies have begun to provide some assistance.

WILDLIFE PROTECTION

In the years since declaring independence, the Azerbaijani people have become increasingly committed to restoring the environment and protecting wildlife. There are now 15 nature reserves, 8 national parks, and 24 restricted natural habitats.

The Persian leopard (*Panthera pardus saxicolor*), also called the Caucasian leopard, lives in several mountainous locations in Azerbaijan, but its numbers are very low.

The protected natural habitats are of special interest because they help safeguard some of the species that are endangered or threatened, like the leopard and the wisent. For example, the Altyaghach National Park protects the only natural habitat for the rare East Caucasian tur, a mountain-dwelling goat antelope.

Azerbaijanis have traditionally been hunters, and there are several popular big-game species, including bears, wild boars, and several kinds of deer, in the country. In addition, visitors from Russia and several other countries find the nature reserves ideal places for hunting, particularly since reserves in many other countries are off-limits to hunters.

Both overhunting and overfishing have created trouble in the past, but in the 21st century, poaching has become a more serious problem. This is especially

The Caspian seal is a marine mammal found only in the sea for which it is named. In fact, it's the only marine mammal in the Caspian, and its population is endangered.

Over the last century, its population has fallen by more than 90 percent, mainly due to hunting and environmental stresses.

Shown here is a Caspian seal (*Pusa caspica*).

Throughout most of the 20th century, the seal was hunted commercially. The Soviet Union—which included four of the five countries now surrounding the Caspian (Russia, Kazakhstan, Turkmenistan, and Azerbaijan)—killed tens of thousands of adult seals and their pups on their ice-breeding grounds and the islands off Azerbaijan. The seals were hunted primarily for their blubber, which was rendered into oil. Then, the soft fur of the seal pups became fashionable, and they were slaughtered in even greater numbers.

Most of the commercial hunting has since ended, but Russia continues to hunt a few thousand seals, mostly pups, every year. In addition, seals are killed around fishing operations, both deliberately to keep them from eating the fish and accidently, such as when they get caught in fishing nets. Pollution of the Caspian waters has also taken its toll on the seal population, causing disease and disrupting the food chain.

A number of small non-governmental environmental organizations in the Caspian countries are working to save the seals from extinction.

true when it comes to the illegal harvesting of Caspian Sea sturgeons. The Convention on International Trade in Endangered Species has listed all varieties of sturgeon as endangered, and the fines for poaching are stiff.

CASPIAN SEA STURGEON

Sturgeon are large, bony, primitive fishes. They are called "primitive" because they date extremely far back in Earth's history—around 208 to 245 million years. Based on the earliest sturgeon fossils, the animals have remained relatively unchanged in all that time.

There are a number of subspecies of sturgeon located throughout the Northern Hemisphere, including several in the Caspian Sea. They range greatly in size, with many species less than 24 inches (61 cm) long and others more than 10 feet (3 m) long and weighing 500 pounds (227 kilograms).

Three or four subspecies of Caspian sturgeon, especially beluga, are prized for their black or gray roe (eggs), which is used for caviar. Adding just the right amount of salt and finding the exact temperature for storing the roe without freezing it are essential for preparing the delicacy. There have been many caviar imitations—the red roe of salmon is sold as "red caviar," and often the

roe of whitefish has been dyed black with the ink of cuttlefish, but true caviar experts are never fooled. Beluga caviar is one of the world's most expensive ingredients.

The Caspian Sea sturgeon is now listed as critically endangered, a result of overfishing and pollution of the Caspian Sea. In 2005, the United States Fish and Wildlife Service banned the importation of beluga caviar from the Caspian Sea and Black Sea basin. That same year, Russia became the first of the Caspian countries to enact an outright ban on catching sturgeon. In 2018, the five Caspian nations agreed to further protections for the sturgeon.

FORESTS

Nearly 12 percent of Azerbaijan is covered in forest, mostly in the mountain regions. Insufficient forest management in the past added to environmental stresses that are now being addressed. For example, illegal commercial logging and the harvesting of trees for firewood by villagers are two of the biggest problems. In addition, climate change is causing an increase in forest fires.

Today, the government is working to improve and sustainably manage the country's forests. It developed a new National Forestry Program initiative for 2020 to 2030 with support from the United Nations Economic Commission for Europe (UNECE). In 2019, Azerbaijan joined the international Bonn Challenge, a global effort to restore 370 million acres (150 million ha) of degraded and deforested land by 2020 and another 350 million acres (142 million ha) by 2030. Azerbaijan committed to restoring 420,000 acres (170,000 ha) of its forests by 2030—and an additional 248,000 acres (100,362 ha) if possible, pending additional funding.

Protecting forests will improve the nation's overall environmental health and add value to Azerbaijan's tourism and recreational facilities.

INTERNET LINKS

https://caspiannews.com/news-detail/nature-parks-of-azerbaijan-2018-3-26-0
This site takes a quick look at five of Azerbaijan's national parks.

https://theculturetrip.com/europe/azerbaijan/articles/beautiful-national-parks-azerbaijan
This travel site offers a quick view of some of the best national parks in the country, with links to other articles.

https://www.vice.com/en_au/article/7x784g/this-city-of-oil-rigs-is-collapsing-into-the-caspian-sea
This 2018 article offers a good overview of the Oil Rocks complex.

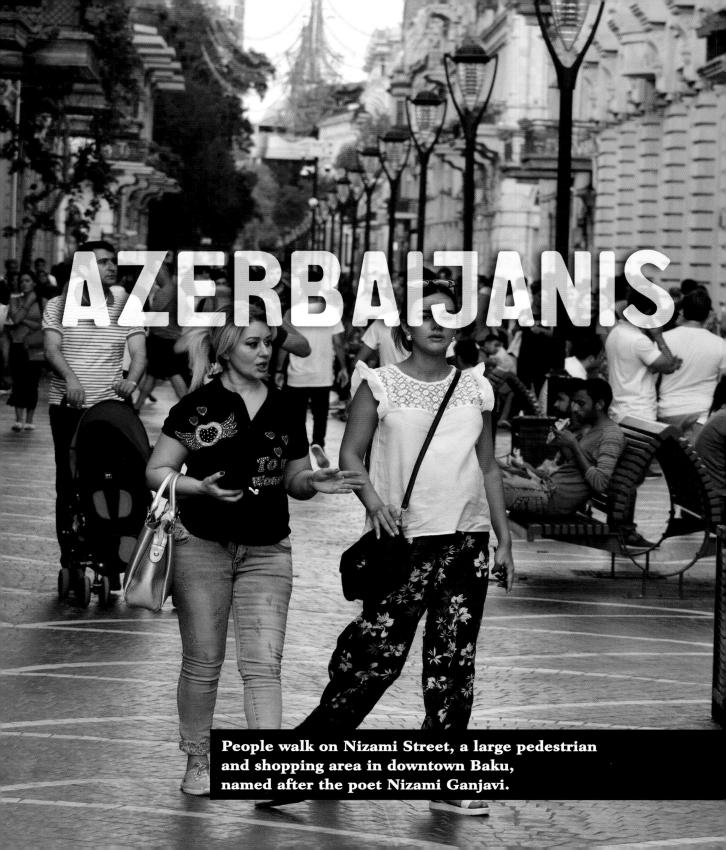

AZERBAIJANIS

People walk on Nizami Street, a large pedestrian
and shopping area in downtown Baku,
named after the poet Nizami Ganjavi.

AZERBAIJANI IS BOTH A NATIONALITY and an ethnicity. The citizens of Azerbaijan are Azerbaijanis. Also, the great majority of Azerbaijanis are ethnic Azerbaijanis, who are also found in neighboring Iran and Dagestan.

Azerbaijan's location at one of the major crossroads between Asia and Europe has led to a remarkable blending of peoples, religions, and languages. This mixing has been continuous since prehistoric times, and it is reflected in the makeup of the nation today, which includes members of more than 70 ethnic groups.

The largest group by far, the ethnic Azerbaijanis or Azeris, constitute more than 90 percent of the country's 10,205,800 people. Other major groups, with rough estimates of their share of the population, include Lezgins (2 percent), Russians (1.3 percent), Armenians (1.3 percent), and Talysh (1.3 percent). Other groups, many of which include only a few thousand people, are Avars, Ukrainians, Tatars, Georgians, and Kurds.

Historic events tend to move people around. For example, after Azerbaijan attained independence, many Russians and other Slavic people moved back to Russia or to other former Soviet republics. This led to a 50 percent reduction in the Russian population of Azerbaijan. Also, since the war over Nagorno-Karabakh, almost all of the Armenians listed as being in Azerbaijan now live in that breakaway republic. The war pitted Azeri Muslims against Armenian Christians. Thousands of Armenians left Azerbaijan for Armenia, both during and after the conflict.

6

The "Baku Process" is a multicultural initiative started by the Republic of Azerbaijan in 2008. It has since grown into a global forum on intercultural dialogue. It brings together political, cultural, and religious leaders for discussions aimed at finding peace, security, tolerance, and understanding of diversity.

Although the large majority of Azerbaijanis are of the same ethnic and religious group, the country considers itself a diverse society. As such, it is committed to the ideals of multiculturalism within the framework of an ideology called Azerbaijanism.

The ideology is essentially a form of nationalism that is meant to unite the diverse peoples of the country under one national identity. Azerbaijanism, therefore, professes the mutual support, cooperation, and equality of its diverse peoples. It also asserts such qualities as nationality, patriotism, loyalty, and the responsibility of the citizen.

This concept arose in the late 19th to early 20th century and was later promoted by the third president of independent Azerbaijan, Heydar Aliyev. "The main idea of the independent Azerbaijani state is Azerbaijanism," Aliyev said in his address to the First Congress of World Azerbaijanis in 2001. "Each Azerbaijani should be proud of his national identity, and we should develop Azerbaijanism—language, culture, national-cultural values, customs, and traditions of Azerbaijan."

An "I Love Baku" sculpture adorns a park in Baku near the Heydar Aliyev Cultural Center, which is in the background.

Aliyev's son and successor, Ilham Aliyev, also embraces the ideology as the basis of Azerbaijan's strength and nationhood. However, some minority groups, such as some of the Talysh people, for example, see it as a way of obliterating their cultures, traditions, and languages.

NOMADS AND CONQUERORS

In the sixth century CE, large bands of nomads traveling by camel and horse swept across the arid steppes of south-central Asia. The Chinese called these people T'uchueh, which has been translated as Turkish. The Turkish bands built

a strong empire that stretched from Mongolia and northern China westward to the Black Sea.

Members of one large Turkish group settled on the western shore of the Caspian Sea, where they mixed with the indigenous population, a group that traced its ancestry back more than 1,000 years to ancient Persia. Over several centuries, the two factions blended into today's Azeri population, with the Turkish culture and language dominant.

From about 600 to 1600 CE, other nomadic groups pushed across the Asian deserts and steppes. Some bands were merchants, traveling in long camel caravans. (It was with such caravans that Marco Polo traveled to the empire of Genghis Khan in China from 1271 to 1295, returning to Europe with tales of the wonders and riches of Asia.) Other bands, including the Huns and Khazars, came westward as conquerors. These warlike groups often uprooted established communities, as whole societies fled the "hordes." This led to

The ruins of a 14-century *caravanserai* (roadside inn), stands in the Gobustan steppes along an ancient trade route.

THE TALYSH SECRET OF LONGEVITY

In the town of Lerik, high in the Talysh Mountains of southeastern Azerbaijan, there is a small museum devoted to longevity. That's because the region has long claimed to be the home of the longest-living people on Earth. The recently renovated museum's exhibits celebrate the lives and memories of the town's many centenarians, past and present.

According to local lore, the Talysh people have regularly lived to be well over a century old. Some, say the locals, lived to be 120, 130, 140 years old, and even older! The oldest resident,

A small village dots the mountainside in Lerik, Azerbaijan.

a shepherd named Shirali Muslumov, who died in 1973, supposedly lived to be 168—at least, according to his passport, which reported his birth year to be 1805.

The locals credit this extraordinary longevity to Lerik's pure mountain air and water; a healthy diet based on lots of yogurt and herbal teas; and good, clean living.

Academic studies on the topic do find that high elevations might help to sustain longer lifespans. However, most scientists who study human longevity believe the extraordinary ages claimed by the Talysh people are impossible and more a result of poor record keeping in the old days. Also, perhaps the culture itself may lead people to believe they are older than they are.

In any event, the high Caucasus region is well known for its "long-lifers." However, perhaps because the stresses of modern life have caught up to the region, it seems that the people aren't living as long as they used to.

more Turkish groups settling in Azerbaijan. North of the Caucasus Mountains, fleeing peoples also pressed into Europe.

One group of conquerors was the Arab Muslims who made the entire region part of the great empire of Islam. The Seljuk Turks took control in the 11th century. Except for about 200 years under Mongol rule, Azerbaijan continued to be dominated by Turkish government and culture.

ETHNIC ENCLAVES

Many of the country's minority groups have tended to live close together, as immigrant groups often do. In Azerbaijan, however, this geographic proximity has, in some cases, continued for centuries. A few of these ethnic groups have also remained quite isolated from the mainstream of society. The Khinalug (or Xinaliq) people, for example, numbering only a few thousand, have continued to live in a cluster of villages high in the Caucasus Mountains. Their customs and language have changed very little since the Middle Ages.

This view of a remote Khinalug village in the Caucasus Mountains shows its isolation.

A Lezgin woman makes traditional bread in Khazra, in the Qusar District in the north of Azerbaijan.

Unlike the Khinalug, most members of minority groups have considerable contact with other minorities, but they still tend to live in identifiable enclaves. Nearly 150,000 Lezgins (also known as Lezghins or Lezghians) live in a number of towns and villages scattered along the northeastern border with Russia and on the southern slopes of the Greater Caucasus Mountains. Many of these towns have two or more neighborhoods in which other minorities live. In addition, about 50,000 Lezgins have moved to Baku and other major cities, but most still consider home to be the town or village where their family members continue to live.

Another significant minority, the Talysh, live in southeastern Azerbaijan near the border with Iran. Like the Azeri population, the Talysh are divided by the Iran-Azerbaijan border, with more than 1 million Talysh living on the Iran side and perhaps half as many residing in Azerbaijan. (Talysh nationalists claim a much higher figure.) Most Talysh live in small towns or in mountain villages, where ancient traditions and handicrafts—including the famous Talysh carpets—have been maintained for hundreds of years. Farmers in the lush semi-tropical valleys operate tea plantations and also have orchards of citrus fruit trees and feijoas, fruit-bearing shrubs. The Talysh people are of Persian ancestry, and they speak an Indo-European language. This sets them apart from the majority of Azerbaijanis, whose background and language are Turkic.

INTERNET LINKS

https://bakuprocess.az/baku-process/about-process
The Baku Process is explained on its official website.

http://multiculturalism.preslib.az/en.htm
The website of the Azerbaijani presidential library provides this section on multiculturalism.

https://unpo.org/members/17338
The Unrepresented Nations and Peoples Organization (UNPO) lists the Talysh people of Azerbaijan and provides related articles.

LIFESTYLE

A shepherd poses with his flock of sheep in a river valley near Mount Shahdag in the Greater Caucasus Mountains.

7

AZERBAIJANI LIFE IS A MIX OF NEW and old. The people are striving to develop their country economically. There is a feeling of energy and excitement, especially in Baku and other cities, where new buildings and new businesses seem to emerge every day.

At the same time, however, there is something relaxed and casual about Azerbaijani life. People still like to take their time over a festive meal or an evening stroll. According to veteran world travelers, Azerbaijan seems like a modern European country in its economic growth and energy but more like a traditional agrarian society in its laid-back lifestyle. Azerbaijanis are often friendly and outgoing, and they are eager to open their homes to outsiders.

The Azerbaijani approach to Islam is also somewhat relaxed. For instance, many Azerbaijanis drink alcohol, a practice that would be forbidden in most other Muslim countries.

Similarly, some Muslim women wear Western-style clothing, while others prefer more traditional Muslim dress. New ideas and new ways of doing things are challenging traditions and forcing people to make rapid adjustments in their attitudes and daily lives.

LIFE IN BAKU

Azerbaijan's capital is a vibrant, growing city—one of the most colorful and exciting in the former Soviet Union. New business centers and office towers rise against a background of ancient palaces, churches, and

In 1918, Azerbaijan became one the first countries to give women the right to vote. It was the first Islamic nation to do so, and it preceded the United States' similar action by two years. Although women's status is far from equal to men's in other ways, women also hold high positions in government and serve in the military.

mosques. In fact, Baku's charm lies in its lively mixture of ancient and modern. In addition to constructing glistening new buildings, there is an ambitious effort to preserve the old. One major restoration project involves repairing the mansions built during the oil boom of the late 1800s.

Baku was built on natural terraces leading down to the deep turquoise of the Caspian Sea. Its physical layout offers many views of outstanding architecture dating back a thousand years. The most remarkable part of the city, for residents and visitors alike, is the magical Old City—Icari Sahar (or Icheri Sheher). This is a walled neighborhood of narrow, twisting cobblestone streets where craftspeople and merchants hawk handcrafted rugs, brassware, copper, ceramics, and antiques. Foreign visitors and Azerbaijani families can spend hours shopping amid the stalls and shops or touring famous historic sites including the carpet museum, the Palace of the Shirvanshahs, and the mysterious Maiden Tower. The entire Old City is listed as a UNESCO World Heritage site.

Outside the walls of the Old City is an area along the shore that residents call simply the *bulva*, or boulevard. This parklike setting is where Bakunian

People walk along a shoreline park in Baku with the Flame Towers rising up behind them.

families come for evening walks. Fountain Square is a popular gathering place where there is a small fairground for children. The Heydar Aliyev Center often hosts special events on its grounds. The recent economic boom in Baku brought plenty for kids to enjoy. Teenagers are drawn to the minicars and motorbikes for rent at Fisherman's Wharf. Also, as an indicator of the region's internationalism, there are 16 McDonald's restaurants in the Baku area or on the Absheron Peninsula.

RURAL LIFE

Nearly half the country's population lives in small towns and farm villages. Although there are many different kinds of farms, including grain and cotton farms, vineyards, and vegetable and livestock farms, rural life tends to follow similar patterns. People rise early and take advantage of the hours of sunlight. Their diet is simple, centering mostly on vegetables, fruit, and milk products such as yogurt. Their normal beverage is spring water, and many drink wine in the evening. Most rural people, including children, bathe almost every day, often in cold rivers or streams. It is said to be an extremely healthy lifestyle, and Azerbaijanis are famous for their long life span.

FAMILY LIFE

People of all ages spend their free time with their family, and this includes the extended family as well as the primary unit of parents and children. Several generations may live together, in both rural and urban settings, and it's common to find grandparents living with their children and grandchildren. Extended families maintain their connections, often coming together for special occasions.

As more people move to Baku and other cities, maintaining those close ties becomes more difficult. When it is time to find a job, however, the urban newcomer is most likely to turn to members of the extended family for help. These kinship ties remain important in matters of personal advancement involving business or politics.

WOMEN AND CHILDREN

The constitution of Azerbaijan prohibits discrimination based on sex and guarantees equal rights for men and women—and husband and wife. That said, the status of women in the country is far from equal to that of men.

Traditionally, women remained at home, caring for the children and the household, while men went to work. In the 21st century, the status of women has been affected by modern perspectives. People in rural areas are much more likely to abide by traditional ways, while people in the cities may embrace a newer outlook. Just like in many other countries today, families may find that the woman needs to work outside the home simply to make financial ends meet.

Women make up about 48 percent of the workforce, but they tend to work in traditionally female professions. Women make up 73.8 percent of workers in the field of education, for example, and 76.5 percent of those working in

A young Azerbaijani family takes a walk in the city. The woman is wearing a white hijab, but the conservative clothing is not mandatory.

THE GENDER GAP

The Global Gender Gap Index for 2020 ranked Azerbaijan in 94th place on a list of 153 countries. The index, created by the World Economic Forum, a not-for-profit foundation based in Geneva, Switzerland, tracks the discrepancies between men and women in four key areas: economics, education, health, and politics. The "gap" refers to the statistical distance between the two genders; the smaller the gap, the closer the genders are to parity, or equality, in a given society. For perspective, the number one country that year, with the smallest gap, was Iceland. The country with the greatest difference, at number 153, was Yemen. The United States ranked number 53.

Globally, women are faring much better in the categories of health and education than they have been historically. In terms of economic opportunity and participation, they are significantly worse off, and in political empowerment, they are the furthest from achieving equality with men.

However, Azerbaijan appears to be an outlier in the category of health and survival, where it ranks 152nd, ahead of only China. This rank, surprising for a middle-income country, is the result of an abnormally wide gap in the number of births of each gender.

The discrepancy reached its heights from 2000 to 2010, when there were about 117 boys born for every 100 girls in Azerbaijan. It has since begun to fall somewhat. Although nature tends to provide for 105 boys per 100 girls at birth, these figures in Azerbaijan are outside the norm. They likely reflect terminated pregnancies based on gender. In other words, pregnant women were more likely to end a pregnancy when they knew the fetus was female—a practice that indicates a strong cultural bias in favor of boys.

health and social services—two sectors that tend to pay lower salaries. Overall, they earn only 50.6 percent of what men earn.

Children's rights are protected by the constitution. Azerbaijan ratified the 1992 UN Convention on the Rights of the Child (CRC) and harmonized its legislation with the principles stated in the CRC in 1998. In 2006, the government established the State Committee for Family, Woman, and Child Issues to monitor compliance.

Despite these legal protections, children do fall through the cracks. Enforcement is not as vigilant as it could be. Several international child protection organizations, including UNICEF, have a presence in the country. They work with the government on issues involving the education and health of children. They tackle specific problems, such as the needs of children with disabilities, the large number of children living on the streets, and violence against children. They also work to prevent early marriages, child labor, and child mortality and improve access to preschool education.

EDUCATION

In the early 20th century, few Azerbaijanis received a formal education. In 1917, only about 10 percent of the people were able to read and write. The picture changed dramatically when the Soviet Union seized control in the early 1920s. Communist authorities placed great importance on education, and they implemented an ambitious program of school construction. By 1959, elementary school was free and compulsory, and 97 percent of the people were literate. In 1966, universal secondary education was introduced, much of it in vocational schools. Russian-language schools were also introduced as the Soviets sought to unify all the republics in their sphere through Russian language and culture.

Azerbaijan now has mandatory schooling for children ages 6 to 17. The state school system is free and secular in character. Most schools are taught in the Azerbaijani language, but some are taught in Russian from the earliest grades right through university. Private schools offer instruction in English and other languages.

Although education is compulsory, in isolated rural areas children may be pulled from school to work on the family farm or in other labor. In very traditional families, education beyond a certain point may not be considered important, and enforcement of school attendance is lax. However, these attitudes are changing as the government and outside organizations work to keep children in school. Azerbaijan wants its people to be well educated, on par with the best of European standards, because a well-educated populace is necessary for top economic performance.

Azerbaijan now has a number of well-respected state and private universities, many of which are in Baku. They include a medical school, a polytechnic institute, music and arts schools, and business schools, as well as institutes for economics, agriculture, languages, and oil and industry.

Schoolchildren work at colorful desks in a classroom in Baku.

INTERNET LINKS

https://www.adb.org/sites/default/files/institutional-document/546166/azerbaijan-country-gender-assessment-2019.pdf
This report provides up-to-date statistical data regarding gender issues in Azerbaijan.

http://azerbaijan24.com/about/people/daily_life
This travel site offers a snapshot of daily life in Azerbaijan.

RELIGION

The Heydar Aliyev Mosque in Baku is the largest mosque in Azerbaijan. Named for the former president and built on the orders of his son, it opened in 2014.

8

AZERBAIJAN IS ONE OF THE MOST liberal Muslim-majority countries. In many Muslim countries, such as neighboring Iran, religious leaders exert a powerful influence over government and society. This is not the case in Azerbaijan, which remains a secular society, controlled by civilian political leaders. In addition, even though more than 90 percent of Azerbaijanis consider themselves Muslims, many do not follow the religion strictly.

The second-largest religious group is made up of the followers of different Christian churches, mostly Eastern Orthodox. They form roughly 3 percent of the population. The Armenian minority, who mostly live in the breakaway republic of Nagorno-Karabakh, are mainly followers of the Armenian Apostolic Church. Other Christians belong to the Russian or the Greek Orthodox churches.

ISLAM

The Prophet Muhammad established Islam around 622 CE in Medina, in what is now Saudi Arabia. Islam means "to submit" in Arabic. A Muslim submits to the will of God (Allah), which was revealed through the

THE FIVE PILLARS OF ISLAM

Five pillars, or requirements, form the basis of Islam. These five pillars, as well as obligations such as being honest, just, and willing to defend Islam and prohibitions against eating pork, drinking alcohol, or lending money for interest or gambling, form common bonds among Muslims. In Azerbaijan, however, the prohibition against alcohol is not necessarily part of the culture. Below are the five pillars and what they mean.

1. Shahada *(sha-ha-DAH)* . . . . *Professing faith in the form of a recitation—"There is no God but Allah, and Muhammad is his prophet."*

2. Salat *(sal-AT)* . . . . *Praying five times a day in the correct manner*

3. Zakat *(za-KAAT)* . . . . . . *Giving alms to the needy or to good causes*

4. Saum *(SOWM)* . . . . *Fasting (not even drinking water) between sunrise and sunset for the 28 days of the Islamic month of Ramadan*

5. Hajj *(HAJ)* . . . . *Making the pilgrimage to Mecca at least once in a lifetime*

prophets—including Abraham, Moses, Jesus, and others recognized in Judaism and Christianity. For Muslims, the last and greatest of these prophets was Muhammad, to whom the Quran (Koran), the word of God, was revealed by the angel Gabriel. The Quran is the holy book of Islam.

Islam was introduced to Azerbaijan in 642 CE, early in the creation of the great Islamic empire, which stretched from Spain in the west across North Africa and Asia to the South Pacific. Shia Islam was made the official religion in the 16th century. Today, however, although Islam is by far the majority religion, it is not the official religion, because there isn't one. The constitution proclaims that Azerbaijan is a secular state.

Islam is divided into two main branches: Shia and Sunni. Worldwide, Sunnis make up the largest Muslim population. However, in Azerbaijan, roughly

85 percent of the people are Shia, and about 15 percent are Sunni. Divisions between the two branches causes trouble in some Muslim countries, but a spirit of tolerance prevails in Azerbaijan. In Baku, for example, many mosques serve both Shia Muslims and Sunnis.

The Rahimah Khanum Mosque in Nardaran is a four-minaret mosque built centuries ago during the Safavid Empire.

RAMADAN

The month of Ramadan is the most holy period in the Islamic year, an observance of the time during which the Koran was revealed to Muhammad. This takes place in the ninth month of the Islamic year, which follows the lunar calendar. So the exact period during which Ramadan is observed is different each year.

Men pray on Eid al-Fitr (the celebration of the end of Ramadan) in the magnificently decorated Mir Movsum Agha Sanctuary in Baku. The sanctuary is named after the "Boneless One," a man who had physical disabilities but who was also believed to have spiritual powers.

Muslims show their obedience to God's will by observing a strict fast from first light in the morning until dark. Part of the day is spent in prayer, both with family members and in a mosque. As soon as it is dark, Azeri Muslims break the fast with family and friends, often with a long meal interspersed with prayer. In Baku and other cities, the festive meal can continue far into the night.

SOVIET RULE AND ISLAM

During the 70 years of Soviet rule, roughly from 1921 to 1991, Communist authorities tried to crush organized religion in all parts of the Soviet empire. In Azerbaijan, the effort to suppress Islam was especially vigorous during the 1930s. Mosques were closed or destroyed, religious leaders were persecuted, and religious observances were officially condemned.

A strong Islamic revival began in the 1980s. In part, this was a way of protesting Soviet rule, but it also represented a desire to return to Islamic traditions.

FEAR OF EXTREMISM

In some Muslim countries, such as Iran, this religious resurgence led to the creation of an Islamic state and a rejection of progressive attitudes such as equal rights for women. For example, in Saudi Arabia, a form of Sunni Islam known as Wahhabism has taken root and led to an increase in religious fundamentalism and extremism.

Shia Muslims can be fundamentalists as well. The Azeri town of Nardaran, on the north shore of the Absheron Peninsula, has long been a center of conservative Shia Islam. Certain foreign entities, primarily Iran, have been said to be importing fundamentalist views into the region.

Since most extremist, militant Muslim movements—such as the Taliban in Afghanistan and Pakistan and the Islamic State, found in Syria, Iraq, and beyond—have grown out of ultra-conservative Islam, the Azerbaijani government tries to discourage such practices.

However, a thin line exists between discouraging certain religious practices and trampling on human rights and the freedom of religion. In 2015, Azerbaijani security services carried out a series of raids in Nardaran, arresting religious activists they accused of plotting to overthrow the government. The raids resulted in at least seven deaths, including five civilians and two policemen.

Following that event, the Azerbaijani parliament passed laws prohibiting people who received religious education abroad from performing religious rites, preaching in mosques, or holding political positions in the country. The laws also prohibit the public display of religious paraphernalia, flags, and slogans, except in places of worship. In addition, the government banned certain seemingly harmful public demonstrations honoring the Muslim holy day of Ashura.

The government is particularly concerned about Azerbaijanis becoming involved in international Islamist extremist movements. As of late 2017, around 900 Azerbaijanis had joined the militant group called the Islamic State (IS or ISIS). New laws will revoke citizenship for any Azerbaijani who does so.

ANCIENT TRADITIONS

In the mountain villages of Azerbaijan, ancient beliefs and traditions are sometimes mixed with Islam. One example of this blending can be witnessed at the mountain called Besh Barmag ("Five-Finger Mountain"), which towers above an ancient trade route in northern Azerbaijan. The summit of Besh Barmag is a *pir*, or holy site. Crowds of visitors make their way up perilous rocky paths to find the holy men, in white robes and caps, each in his own rocky nook marked only by a few blankets, fluttering ribbons, and an urn used for tea called a samovar. The people come hoping to have a special wish granted, such as wanting good health, a child, or good fortune. The holy men chant prayers and dispense bits of wisdom that combine elements of Islam and ancient beliefs such as animism—the idea that there are spirits in all natural objects and events.

ZOROASTRIAN INFLUENCES

Similar holy places are scattered throughout Azerbaijan, especially in the mountains. Some of these include elements of Zoroastrianism, an ancient Persian religion (c. 600 BCE—650 CE) that spread from Iran and Azerbaijan to India.

Zoroaster was a priest in ancient Persia (Iran) who developed an elaborate theology of monotheism, or belief in one god. Jews and Christians regarded him as an astrologer, mathematician, prophet, and a major heretic. When Azerbaijan and Persia became Muslim, Zoroastrianism was tolerated for about 300 years, but then persecution led most followers to flee to India.

One of the beliefs of Zoroastrianism that has been integrated into a few small Azerbaijani sects is that Zoroaster carried sacred fires to many parts of the world. Fire is the most important symbol of purity in the religion. Zoroastrians worshipped fire and believed it represented the holy spirit of Ahura Mazda, the creator.

There are many places in Azerbaijan where jets of natural gas have created long-lasting flames. Architectural ruins and other cultural remnants from

Zoroaster, also called Zarathustra, was a priest in Persia, but the dates of his life are uncertain. Scholars date his existence as being anywhere from 1500 BCE to 650 BCE or so. Not much is known about him or his life, but he had a powerful effect on history. He lived in a time when most religions were polytheistic; that is, people believed in many different gods. Zoroaster worked out a complex philosophy and religion based, instead, on monotheism, the belief in one god. He also developed the concept of dualism in religion—the belief that the universe is controlled by two forces—Good and Evil. This belief system influenced the development of Judaism, Christianity, and Islam.

This wall sculpture in Mumbai, India, depicts Zoroaster.

Zoroaster is also said to have been one of the originators of astrology, the practice of reading cosmic signs as a way of predicting future events, and he is believed to have had a hand in developing the field of magic. He also influenced classical civilization in ancient Greece. The Greeks considered him a skilled healer, craftsman, and agriculturist, as well as an esteemed philosopher, mathematician, astrologer, and magician.

The Zoroastrian faith became the main religion of Persia (present-day Iran) until the emergence of Islam in the seventh century CE. Muslim persecution soon forced followers of the religion to flee. The largest numbers migrated to India where, in the Mumbai (formerly Bombay) region, they developed into a well-educated, wealthy community known as the Parsees. Gradually, after 1800, small groups of Zoroastrians began to move back to Iran, while some, moving farther north into Azerbaijan, found the keepers of the temple flames still at their posts in the Ateshgah Fire Temple on the Absheron Peninsula. The remnants of Zoroastrianism that exist today are just one example of the mysterious mixing of folk beliefs and ancient religions found throughout Azerbaijan.

the era of Zoroastrianism in Azerbaijan are found throughout the country. Some have been preserved. In Baku, the ancient Walled City, a UNESCO World Heritage site, reveals evidence of Zoroastrian culture.

The Baku Ateshgah ("Fire Temple of Baku") in the Baku suburb of Suraxani was built over one of these jets where, it is said, the flame has been sustained for more than 1,200 years. However, the natural flame died in 1969 and is now lit by gas piped in for this purpose. Some Zoroastrians continue to maintain the temple.

One of the most important legacies of Zoroastrianism is the Nowruz spring festival, which is said to have been founded by Zoroaster himself. The four Tuesdays leading up to the holiday celebrate the four elements—water, fire, earth, and wind. One of the beloved Nowruz customs is that of leaping over bonfires, another nod to the festival's Zoroastrian, fire-worshipping roots.

A person jumps over a bonfire as part of the Nowruz celebrations, marking the arrival of spring in Baku on March 17, 2020.

JEWS

Jews make up a small percentage of the country's population. About half of the nation's Jews live in a few mountain towns across the Kudyal River from the small city of Quba in northeastern Azerbaijan. These are the so-called Mountain Jews. They have lived in this region for many centuries.

Some legends associate them with the biblical figure Noah, while others depict them as one of the lost tribes of Israel. Through isolation, their language has separated from the nation's Turkic into an Indo-European language called Judeo-Tat. The Mountain Jews have generally lived in peace with other groups, although they have been persecuted at times in the past.

The other Azerbaijani Jews live in the cities, especially Baku. Many have professional or administrative positions. The Jewish population has been declining steadily since about 1990, largely in reaction to world events. The breakup of the Soviet Union led several thousand Jews to emigrate, for example, mostly from Baku to Israel. The mid-1990s warfare in Nagorno-Karabakh caused many more to leave. The number of Jews in Azerbaijan has now declined to about 30,000.

INTERNET LINKS

https://www.ancient.eu/zoroastrianism
The Ancient History Encyclopedia provides information about Zoroaster and the religion named for him.

https://www.azconsulatela.org/Azerbaijan/Religion-and-Religious-Tolerance
An Azerbaijani consular site offers this overview of religion in the country.

https://www.ijn.com/letter-from-azerbaijan-jewish-life-in-the-muslim-country-flourishes
This article looks at Jewish life in Azerbaijan today.

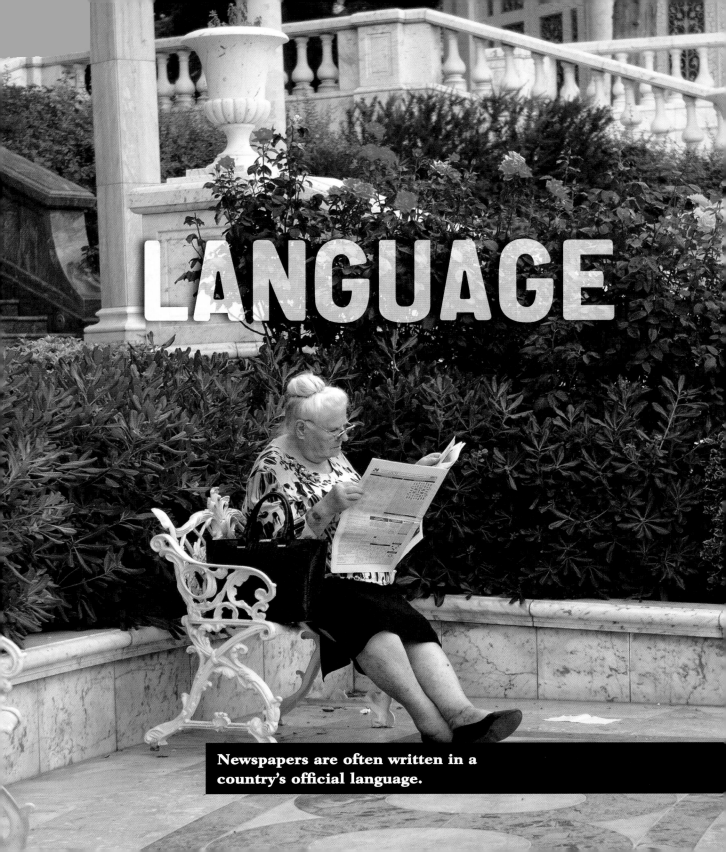

LANGUAGE

Newspapers are often written in a country's official language.

MORE THAN 90 PERCENT OF Azerbaijan's population speaks Azerbaijani, or Azeri, which is part of a language family known as Turkic. Azeri shares much of its grammar and vocabulary with Turkish. In fact, a visitor from Turkey could travel through Azerbaijan with only a few language difficulties.

The written form of Azeri has gone through several fundamental changes. Originally, it was written in a modified form of Arabic script. In 1918, when Azerbaijan enjoyed its first brief period of independence, the Arabic was quickly replaced with a Latin alphabet similar to one being used at that time in Turkey. In 1939, the Communist government of the Soviet Union ordered the use of the Cyrillic alphabet. This remained the law until 1991, when a revived Azeri Latin alphabet was restored.

Many Azerbaijanis also speak Russian, especially older people who grew up under Soviet rule, when Russian was commonly taught in schools. Since independence, English has become increasingly popular. However, by no means does everyone speak or understand English.

In addition, there are more than 20 other languages spoken by ethnic minorities, and most of these cannot be understood by speakers of Azeri. In the Middle Ages, Arab geographers called the Caucasus Mountains *jebel al alsine*, "the mountain of languages," because there were so many different languages, dialects, and alphabets. Arabic, Latin, and Cyrillic were in use. Today, some of the less common languages and dialects, such

Turkish and Azerbaijani language speakers have 85 to 90 percent intelligibility, which means they can understand each other fairly well.

as Talysh and Lezgi, are spoken by more than 100,000 people in Azerbaijan. Others, such as Rutul, Tabassaran, and Dargwa, are known to only a few thousand people, who firmly insist on their right to preserve their cultures, including their languages.

HISTORIC INFLUENCES

Many of today's languages had their origins centuries ago in the lands of eastern Asia. One family of languages, known as the Altaic languages, began east of the Altai Mountains, an imposing mountain range in central Asia. When nomadic groups moved out of Manchuria and northern China, they carried their languages and customs with them. Three major language groups, all part of the Altaic family, spread in that way: the Mongolian, the Manchu-Tungusic (in China), and the Turkic.

The groups speaking various Turkic languages moved westward, some settling in Azerbaijan, some setting down roots in other areas, including Turkey. Still other bands of nomads spread different groups of languages such as Indo-European, Caucasian, and Iranian.

The relative isolation of various groups has also influenced the development of language in Azerbaijan. Groups such as the Lezgians and Dagestanis spoke East Caucasian languages, and other groups such as the Talysh and Kurds spoke Indo-European languages. As these groups became isolated from the others, especially in mountainous regions, their languages tended to change little, unless there was significant contact with traders from other language groups.

The result of this linguistic isolation is that some of the languages spoken in Azerbaijan have almost nothing in common with one another or with Azeri. Azerbaijan's Armenian minority, for example, speaks an Indo-European language heavily influenced by Persian. Not only is the spoken Armenian impossible for Azeri speakers to understand, but the written form and alphabet, created by a religious leader in the fifth century, compound the problems of translation. In addition, some words or pronunciations may be understandable only to people of a certain village or mountain valley.

Another minority language, Georgian, is related to the Caucasian languages and is one of a group that has no connection to any other linguistic group. An even smaller isolated minority is the village of Khinalug in the rugged northern mountains. The village has been isolated since the Middle Ages, and the language spoken by the population of about 2,000 cannot be understood by outsiders.

THE ALPHABET

The written scripts used by Azerbaijanis bear the mark of the external cultural influences that Azerbaijan has been subject to throughout history. In Azerbaijan, there are several types of alphabets and scripts that are still in use today. The Arabic script, the Russian Cyrillic alphabet, the modern Azeri alphabet, and the Georgian alphabet are some of the major examples.

The Azeri alphabet contains 32 letters. This is an approximation of the sounds associated with the Azeri letters. Those without descriptions make sounds like the English equivalent.

A a . . . . .a *(ah) as in* army	K k . . . .k *or* ch
B b	Q q . . . . .g *as in* gold
C c . . . .j *as in* judge	L l
Ç ç . . . .ch *as in* child	M m
D d	N n
E e . . . .e *as in* eh	O o . . . .o *as in* clock
Ə ə *or* Ä ä . .a *as in* cat	Ö ö . . . .*between* uh *and* oh
F f	P p
G g . . . .*hard* g, *as in* guard	R r . . . .*trilled*
Ğ ğ. . . . .*no similar sound in English; a rough sound deep in throat; no words start with this letter*	S s
	Ş ş . . . .sh
	T t
H h	U u . . . .oo
X x . . . .*hard* ch *as in* loch	Ü ü . . . .ew
I ı . . . . .i *as in* timber	V v
İ i . . . . .ee	Y y
J j . . . .zh *as in* deja vu	Z z

When the Azerbaijani government made the Azeri Latin script the official alphabet in 1991, Azerbaijanis who had been taught the Cyrillic version had to familiarize themselves with the new script. The script was slightly revised again in 1992, changing the letter Ää to Ə ə. This vowel makes a sound something like the æ sound, *a* as in *cat*.

With the rise of electronic media in more recent years, this has become a problem, as most Latin alphabet keyboards do not have the letter ə. Ä is found much more commonly in other languages; therefore when ə is not available, Azeris will use ä.

PRONUNCIATION

Azeri words are usually stressed on the last syllable, but the stress is light. There are many regional variations in pronunciation. In some parts of the country, for example, the hard *k* is pronounced more like a *ch*, so that *baki* is pronounced like "ba-chuh" and *seki* is "sha-chee." *V* is pronounced as in English, except when following a vowel. Then, it makes a *w* sound.

INTERNET LINKS

http://multiculturalism.preslib.az/en_a3.html
This article discusses the various languages of Azerbaijan's diverse peoples.

https://www.omniglot.com/writing/azeri.htm
This language site presents an introduction to Azerbaijani.

https://theculturetrip.com/europe/azerbaijan/articles/21-essential-phrases-youll-need-in-azerbaijan
https://theculturetrip.com/europe/azerbaijan/articles/guide-azerbaijani-language
These two guides to the Azeri language are helpful for travelers.

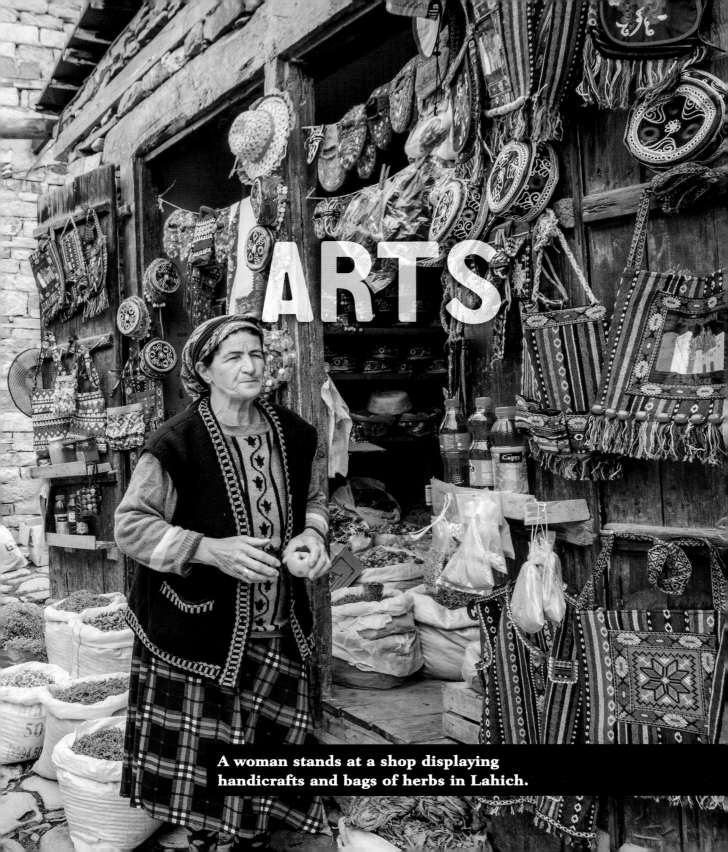

ARTS

A woman stands at a shop displaying handicrafts and bags of herbs in Lahich.

10

JUST AS AZERBAIJAN SPANS BOTH Asia and Europe, its arts reflect the influences of East and West. The Islamic presence is evident today in the great old architecture of Baku and a few other cities, as well as in early literary forms, especially poetry.

The European influence came later, following the completion of Russia's conquests in 1828. One of the greatest Azeri literary figures, Mirza Fatali Akhundov (1812—1878) became central in introducing Western literature and drama. The new literature was concerned with spreading the ideas of the European Enlightenment, with a stress on individual rights and freedoms, gaining knowledge by reason rather than by religious revelation, and the importance of education. These ideas were secular and were designed to reduce the influence of religion.

The early 20th century brought another wave of change to the arts in Azerbaijan. A series of upheavals in Turkey, called the Young Turk Revolution (1908—1909), wrenched that country out of a sleepy, conservative past. The aim of the revolt was to create a modern, Western-style country, including the adoption of European styles of clothing, literature, music, and other elements of culture. In Azerbaijan, the intelligentsia, who were mostly based in Baku, became the leaders in developing the nation's more modern forms of literature and art.

As is true in most Muslim nations, painting never developed as a traditional art form in Azerbaijan. This may be because of an Islamic ban on recreating the human form, a role that is reserved for Allah. Globally, the highest expression of Islamic art is seen in mosque architecture and decoration.

Today, Azerbaijani artists work in Western-style arts as well, especially in Baku, and paintings are exhibited in galleries and museums.

The people who lived in the Azerbaijan region many thousands of years ago left behind evidence of their culture. Rock carvings in the Gobustan area date back around 5,000 to 20,000 years. Among the thousands of images are pictures of humans, animals, boats, camel caravans, ritual dances, war and hunting scenes, and heavenly bodies. The engravings, called petroglyphs, were produced over the course of many thousands of years, from prehistoric periods on up to the Middle Ages.

Gobustan is a rocky, hilly area around 40 miles (64 km) southwest of Baku, near the Caspian Sea. In 1966, the region was declared a national park, and its ancient treasures came under the protection of the government. It also features the remains of inhabited caves, settlements, and burial sites. In addition, the area has an abundance of mud volcanoes. The park, which is open to the public, also has a newly renovated museum.

In 2007, around 1,327 acres (537 ha) of the larger national park was listed as a UNESCO World Heritage site: the Gobustan Rock Art Cultural Landscape. In 2013, it was granted further protections under the Second Protocol of the Hague Convention for the Protection of Cultural Property in the Event of Armed Conflict. This stipulates that the property may not be used for military purposes.

LITERATURE

The different kinds and phases of literary expression in Azerbaijan—folktales, classical Islamic poetry, and modern literature—are considered outstanding examples of creativity. For example, the works of the Persian epic poet Nizami,

or Nezami (c. 1141—1209), are regarded as among the finest ever written in the Persian language.

In Ganja, a sculpture garden depicts the poet Nizami Ganjavi with some of the characters from his works.

He is often called Nizami Ganjavi, named for his place of birth, Ganja. He is also referred to as Hakim ("the Sage"). In rhyming couplets, he produced long dramatic tales of love and heroism. His most famous epic, called the *Khamsa* ("The Quintet"), consists of five romantic masterpieces, called the "Five Treasures." Nizami is greatly revered in Azerbaijan. Almost every town has a statue of him, and there is often a street named after him as well. In Baku, the Nizami Museum of Literature was established in 1939. The poet's mausoleum stands in Ganja, where the parklike grounds feature gardens and statues.

Modern Azeri literature emerged in the 19th century, following the Russian conquest. Even the greatest of the new writers, Mirza Fatali Akhundov, was influenced by Nizami. Akhundov introduced drama in the mid-1800s, believing that this was the best way to convey ideas to a public that was largely illiterate. He wrote biting satires, exposing the social ills of the times.

Two followers of Akhundov—Najaf bey Vazirov and Abdurrahim bey Hagverdiyev—wrote tragic dramas. By the early 1900s, professional theater had become a major form of public entertainment. Azerbaijani literature and theater also influenced Turkey and other countries. During this flowering of the country's culture, the first Azerbaijani opera, *Leyli and Majnun*, based on the poem by Nizami, added a vital new element to the country's arts.

THE SOVIET PERIOD

The period of Soviet rule that began in the 1920s brought major changes to Azeri literature and the arts. The communist campaign for literacy produced a new generation of readers. At the same time, however, Soviet dictator Joseph Stalin was ruthless in suppressing dissent. Some of the most talented Azeri writers were persecuted, and their books were banned. Literature was restricted to "Soviet realism," novels and stories depicting the triumph of the workers over the hated capitalists. All other forms of literary expression were stifled by Stalin's government. In the period just before the 1921 Soviet takeover, 63 newspapers and magazines were in circulation. All but a handful were forced to stop publication, although several tried to continue covertly.

The late 1980s witnessed a sharp change in Soviet control when then-President Mikhail Gorbachev introduced the policy of *glasnost*, or "openness." Writers whose works had been banned saw their creations and their reputations restored. This was accompanied by a great literary revival in which young men and women once again feverishly produced poetry, novels, short fiction, drama, and a variety of journals and magazines. After independence, it was expected that even greater freedom would flourish.

CENSORSHIP

According to the constitution, state censorship is illegal in Azerbaijan, but that has not stopped the government from instituting increasingly greater restrictions on the arts and the media. According to international press freedom

The acclaimed writer Akram Aylisli was well-loved in Azerbaijan and honored as the "People's Writer"—that is, until he published a trilogy of novellas, beginning with Stone Dreams *in 2012. The story deals with interactions between Azerbaijanis and Armenians living in Baku in 1990. It portrays Armenians—subjected to violence at the hands of*

Azerbaijanis—in a sympathetic light. The second book, A Fantastical Traffic Jam, *depicts a brutal dictator who is said to closely resemble Heydar Aliyev, the father of current president Ilham Aliyev.*

Although the books have not been published in the Azeri language, Aylisli has been harassed, threatened with violence, charged with dubious crimes, and put under house arrest. Outraged mobs burned his books, his works were removed from school curricula, and his plays were banned. His wife and son both lost their jobs. A pro-government politician publicly offered $13,000 for someone to cut off one of the author's ears.

Numerous international arts and human rights organizations have taken up Aylisli's cause. It's seen as a prime example of government censorship of the arts and press in this nominally democratic country. Above, Aylisli is pictured during a 2013 interview in Baku.

organizations, President Ilham Aliyev has been relentlessly cracking down on his critics. In its 2019 World Press Freedom Index, Reporters Without Borders ranked Azerbaijan 166th out of 180 nations. In that index, number 1 (Norway) is the nation that enjoys the greatest degree of press freedom, and Turkmenistan, number 180, had the least freedom.

Another organization, Freedom House, had a similar report, assigning Azerbaijan the label of "Not Free" with a score of 0 on the question of a free and independent media. The report adds that artistic expression is similarly subject to political restrictions and details the police beatings of a rapper and a blogger who dared defy the government.

MUSIC AND DANCE

As with many art forms, Azerbaijani music builds on folk traditions that reach back many centuries. In times past, traveling poet-singers called *ashugs* made their living by performing at weddings and public functions. In poetry and song, they recounted the deeds of ancient heroes, usually strumming a stringed instrument called a *kobuz*.

The ashugs often competed with one another in contests that were much like the competitions held among wandering poets in medieval Europe. The Azerbaijani contests rewarded improvisation in both words and music, and this led to a musical form called *mugam*, a style that is still popular today. Like jazz, mugam is varied, with different forms used to convey different feelings or moods. An echo of the ashugs is found in mugam song cycles with texts based on classical poetry.

Azerbaijan's traditional musical instruments include the *kamancha*, seen in the front center left position with its bow, and the keyhole-shaped *tar*, center right.

"Mugam" also refers to the traditional trio that performs the music. Most mugams consist of a singer, a *kamancha* player, and a *tar* player. Both the tar and the kamancha are stringed instruments. The tar has a keyhole-shaped opening, and the strings are plucked. The kamancha has a round opening and its strings are made of horsehair or silk; the sounding board is made of gazelle hide. Public performances of mugam are a popular form of entertainment, and clever improvisations receive the most enthusiastic applause.

An group of Azerbaijani folk musicians and dancers pose at an international folk festival in Masalli.

Jazz became popular late in the Baku oil-boom days as an import from the United States in the 1920s. In the 1950s, a jazz pianist from Baku named Vagif Mustafazade began mixing mugam improvisations with jazz elements to produce a new sound called mugam jazz. His daughter Aziza continued to develop mugam jazz, and her recordings—combined with European tours—have won her an international following.

As in music, folk traditions in dance remain extremely popular. Tours by professional groups and performances by local amateur groups are still the most popular forms of public entertainment. The music, the costumes, and the dance forms are stylized re-creations of ancient traditions. *Lesginka*, for example, is a popular dance developed in the Middle Ages among the Lezgian people in the northern mountains.

The dance begins with a man performing alone, wearing the costume of a mountain warrior and often brandishing a sword. A woman enters, and the male dances to attract her with concise steps and forceful arm movements. The woman dances quietly around him until he finally wins her over. The entire dance takes 10 to 15 minutes and is immediately followed by other short stories in movement.

FOLK ARTS

Like many other western Asian nations, Azerbaijan has a reputation for great artistic skill in handicrafts. While the country is best known for its handwoven rugs, Azerbaijan's craftspeople also produce outstanding pottery, ceramics, metalwork, and calligraphy.

Most artistic styles and techniques are heavily influenced by Persian and early Islamic art. Since Islamic law banned the artistic depiction of humans, Azeris acquired extraordinary skill in detailed ornamentation and abstract design. Craft workers near the Iranian border became famous for manuscript illumination, applying rich and detailed ornamentation to miniature paintings.

Azerbaijan is best known for its variety of textiles, including rugs, carpets, shawls, veils, and towels. Small handwoven rugs differ in design from region to region. Dagestan rugs, for example, feature a short wool pile, with weft

An array of brightly colored carpets is displayed at the Carpet Museum in Baku.

Just as UNESCO (the United Nations Educational, Scientific, and Cultural Organization) works to protect natural and cultural World Heritage sites, it also identifies examples of "Intangible Cultural Heritage of Humanity" that need to be preserved. These include, according to the group's website, "traditions or living expressions inherited from our ancestors and passed on to our descendants, such as oral traditions, performing arts, social practices, rituals, arts, festive events, knowledge and practices concerning nature and the universe or the knowledge and skills to produce traditional crafts."

The Convention for the Safeguarding of the Intangible Cultural Heritage has listed 13 entries for Azerbaijan. These include several musical forms, instruments, dances, folktales, the craft of carpet weaving, silk headscarves, the preparation of dolma and flatbread, and the celebration of Nowruz—the Islamic New Year.

An Azerbaijani woman prepares dolma, or stuffed grape leaves, which is a tradition of Intangible Cultural Heritage.

threads often of cotton. The highly detailed geometric designs create the impression of brightly colored mosaics. Rugs from other regions might include highly stylized images of pheasants, peacocks, flowers, or animals.

Azeri crafts also feature embroidered textiles. They use brightly colored threads—occasionally of gold or silver—as well as tiny beads to create designs on a thin wool fabric called *tirme*. Geometric patterns are common, but colorful birds and other animals are also often featured.

ARCHITECTURE

Azerbaijan's architecture reflects various styles that have changed throughout history. There are scattered ruins, as well as fragments and artifacts that date back to prehistoric times. There are also relics from the Zoroastrian period and the era of the Roman Empire (including graffiti written by a lonely Roman soldier unhappy at being assigned to such a remote outpost).

The ruins of Chirag Gala fortress, built in the fifth century by the Sassanid Persians, was once used as a lookout post for the defense of the Quba khanate.

MODERN ARCHITECTURE

In addition to its ancient treasures, Baku is also home to some marvels of ultra-modern architecture. One of the most recognizable is the Flame Towers complex, which was completed in 2012. The three silver towers soar high above the surrounding cityscape. Inside, one tower contains residential apartments, one has business offices, and one is a hotel. Outside, they are covered in LED screens that

are illuminated at night with the flickering of giant flames and a variety of other lighting effects. The flames represent the wealth generated by the natural gas reserves that fuel the Azerbaijani economy and also the nation's identity as the Land of Fire.

The Heydar Aliyev Center, which also opened in 2012, is a swirling form of wavy lines. The national cultural center, named for the former president, includes a museum, exhibition halls, an auditorium, and a library. It was Heydar Aliyev who first envisioned making Baku into a center of modern architecture. The now-iconic building bearing his name was designed by the Iraqi-British architect Zaha Hadid (1950–2016), one of the world's most acclaimed architects.

The Azerbaijan National Carpet Museum, which opened in 2014, is the whimsical shape of a rolled carpet, complete with geometrical patterns. The building celebrates Azerbaijan's traditional art of carpet weaving, which was inducted into the UNESCO Representative List of the Intangible Cultural Heritage of Humanity in 2010.

The most impressive architecture comes from the long Islamic period. Islamic structures include mosques, minarets (the towers from which the muezzin issues the call to prayer five times a day), mausoleums, palaces, *caravanserai* (roadside inns from the days of the camel caravans), and madrassas (centers of Islamic learning).

One of the most famous buildings is the Maiden Tower in Baku. This sturdy, oval-shaped fortress is eight stories high, with stairways carved into the thick walls. It was started as a defensive tower in the seventh or eighth century and completed in the 12th century. No one knows exactly how the structure got its name or why a door on the third floor opens onto thin air. Baku's walled Old City contains other architectural wonders, including the 15th-century Palace of the Shirvanshahs, which was carefully restored in 2003. The "Walled City of Baku with the Shirvanshah's Palace and Maiden Tower" comprise a single World Heritage site.

The mansions of the 19th-century oil barons are favorite tourist attractions, even though some of the buildings are in disrepair. Baku's subway stations,

The Maiden Tower, also known as Giz Galasi, is a legendary landmark of Baku.

built during the Soviet period, are considered the most successful examples of communist-style architecture. Other Soviet buildings were usually massive concrete public buildings and imposing blocks of apartment buildings. Some Soviet buildings have been partially submerged by the rising waters of the Caspian Sea.

INTERNET LINKS

https://freedomhouse.org/country/azerbaijan/freedom-world/2020
Freedom House reports on media freedom in Azerbaijan.

https://ich.unesco.org/en/state/azerbaijan-AZ
The Intangible Cultural Heritage site for Azerbaijan has links to its listed elements.

https://pen.org/advocacy-case/akram-aylisli
Pen America features the case of persecuted writer Akram Aylisli.

https://rsf.org/en/azerbaijan
Reporters Without Borders evaluates freedom of expression in Azerbaijan.

https://www.travelawaits.com/2486059/stunning-azerbaijan-architecture
The travel site features a quick look at some of Baku's beautiful buildings.

https://whc.unesco.org/en/list/958
This is the World Heritage listing for the Walled City of Baku with the Shirvanshahs' Palace and Maiden Tower.

https://whc.unesco.org/en/list/1076
The World Heritage listing for the Gobustan Rock Art Cultural Landscape is described on this page.

LEISURE

The seaside Primorsky Boulevard in
Baku features a Ferris wheel.

11

L EISURE TIME IS TEA TIME IN Azerbaijan. For rest, relaxation, and companionship, nothing beats a cup of tea, unless it's many cups of tea. For almost any occasion, tea is the perfect drink. In fact, tea is more than a drink in this country; it's a gesture of hospitality and culture and an almost sacred tradition.

Tea, called *chay*, is often served from a samovar, a metal urn with a spigot. It's poured into pear-shaped glasses called *armuda*. Little snacks and special jams may also be offered. The hot tea is never served with milk but always with a sugar cube. The sugar doesn't go into the tea, however. It's placed in the mouth and the tea is sipped through the cube. When guests come to visit, a host will offer tea immediately, no matter the time of day. To not offer tea to a visitor in Azerbaijan would be an insult and the height of inappropriate behavior.

Outside the home, people may gather at teahouses called *chaykhana*. Traditionally, the chaykhana is a place for men to gather to play backgammon, read newspapers, or discuss politics. Women typically visit and drink tea in their homes rather than in public, at least according to custom.

FAMILY TIME

The people of Azerbaijan are family oriented, and leisure time is usually family time. The pace is generally relaxed and easygoing. Evenings are

In 2016, Azerbaijan became one of only two nations (the other being Great Britain, also between 2000 and 2016) to earn an increasing number of medals in five consecutive Olympic Games.

Kids play chess at a festival on the grounds of the Heydar Aliyev Center in Baku.

often spent outdoors, talking, playing chess, or, as rural villagers like to say, "just watching the world go by."

Urban dwellers enjoy evening and weekend strolls. Some of the main shopping areas are closed to traffic, enabling people to walk and talk freely. Every city and town offers a wide variety of shops for items such as carpets, embroidery, copperware, and ceramics. Baku's shopping centers include designer stores with luxury items from Paris, Rome, London, and New York.

Restaurants are great gathering places for social occasions such as weddings, birthdays, and holidays. Family and friends are likely to spend several hours at a festive meal, often accompanied by loud music. Wedding feasts are a favorite social event.

THE MOST POPULAR SPORT

Football—or soccer as it's known in the United States—is indisputably the most popular sport in Azerbaijan. The love of soccer goes back to the early part of the 20th century and has continued without abating. Today, the country has

both a men's and women's national team and several youth teams as well. The national teams represent the country in international competitions, but they have yet to qualify for the World Cup or European Championships.

At home, the teams play at Baku Olympic Stadium, a 68,700-seat venue which opened in 2015. It's the largest stadium in the country.

Young people kick a soccer ball along the streets of Icheri Sheher ("Old City") in Baku.

SEASONAL ACTIVITIES

Azerbaijan has great potential for outdoor activities. It possesses spectacular scenery, and its towering mountains and rugged hills are ideal for skiing. The Caspian Sea's long coastline makes it ideal for summer sports. Since Azerbaijanis gained independence, however, they have been slow to take advantage of the possibilities, largely because of the warfare and economic upheaval that overshadowed much of the 1990s.

A number of obstacles have to be overcome in order for the country to develop its recreational facilities. There is a growing interest in skiing, for example, but there are few facilities. The Tufanagh Winter-Summer Mountain

Resort in Gabala offers year-round activities, with paragliding and trekking in the summer. The Shahdag Mountain Resort in Qusar has 18 ski slopes and state-of-the-art lifts and gondolas. It also offers summer recreation, such as zip-lining, mountain biking, and more. These two resorts are an example of the possibilities that Azerbaijan's mountainous regions might offer with further development.

Summer activities elsewhere include swimming in the Caspian Sea. However, the beaches in the region of the Absheron Peninsula suffer from serious oil pollution and inadequately treated industrial and municipal sewage. Beaches north or south of the peninsula attract more people. Pollution also limits water sports such as sailing, boating, and waterskiing, and some people say they do not like the obstacle course created by oil derricks.

Hiking, mountaineering, and hunting continue to be popular activities. Although Azerbaijan has several snowcapped peaks, there are few approaches for climbers. However, hiking through the rugged hills and mountains attracts a growing number of foreign visitors as well as locals. Many hikers hire local villagers to guide them through mountain passes.

HEALTH RESORTS

During the Soviet era, Azerbaijan had numerous vacation resorts called sanatoriums. These were state-run facilities where workers from factories throughout the Soviet Union could come for a week or two of rest and recreation.

There were also less elaborate vacation places called turbazas. These usually consisted of clusters of cabins in forest areas or near lakes. Both sanatoriums and turbazas were often built next to natural hot springs.

Today, there are a number of historic and updated health spas. One of Azerbaijan's most famous is the Naftalan Resort, which focuses on the therapeutic use of the region's crude oil. Guests bathe in the warm, thick black oil, which is said to help more than 70 skin, joint, and bone diseases. It's used as a disinfectant, an anti-inflammatory treatment, and even an anesthetic.

BOARD GAMES

Many Azerbaijanis are fascinated by two of the world's most ancient board games—chess and *nard*, or backgammon. Both games are played by all ages, and it is said that kids would rather play nard than watch television.

CHESS In 1985, Baku native Garry Kasparov became, at 22, the youngest world chess champion in history. Kasparov remained champion until 2000, when he lost to Russian Vladimir Kramnik. In his 15 years as world champion, the only time Kasparov lost a match was in 1997, when he was beaten by an IBM computer nicknamed Deep Blue. Kasparov's amazing record and his bold style of play heightened the great popularity of chess among Azerbaijanis.

Residents of Baku play nard, or backgammon, on the street.

NARD The board game called nard, or backgammon, is even more popular than chess and can probably be considered the nation's favorite recreational activity. The object of this two-player game is to move your pieces through the four parts of the board before your opponent does. Although the number of spaces moved depends on a roll of the dice, the game is an exciting combination of luck and skill. Each player, for example, can block the other or can force an opponent's game piece back to the start.

People of all ages can spend hours playing nard and practicing new strategies. In every café, there are bound to be several pairs of people playing the game, usually while they have their tea and jam. It is not unusual for a foreign visitor to be invited to play nard even if they do not speak a word of Azeri.

AN ANCIENT SPORT

The ancient game of chovqan, *a game similar to polo, is so treasured that it is on the UNESCO list of Intangible Cultural Heritage. The sport dates back more than a thousand years and is pictured in Persian miniature paintings; it's also mentioned in a poem by the great Nizami.*

In Azerbaijan today, chovqan is considered a national sport. Two teams of six men each, all on horseback, try to score goals by hitting a ball with a stick also called a chovqan. The players wear traditional hats and long coats. The horses are specially trained Karabakh horses, which have just the right size, agility, and temperament for the sport.

During the Soviet era, however, the sport fell out of favor, and fewer young people learned how to play it. Fewer Karabakh horses were raised for the purpose. The sport itself became so endangered that in 2013, it was added to the list of Intangible Cultural Heritage in Need of Urgent Safeguarding.

Men play chovqan against a background of green mountains.

INTERNATIONAL COMPETITION

When Azerbaijani athletes are engaged in international competition, they give the nation a chance to express its tremendous pride. In 1996, for example, 23 athletes traveled to Atlanta, Georgia, for the Summer Olympic Games. This was the first independent Azerbaijani Olympic team, and the athletes were treated as national heroes, especially when wrestler Namig Abdullayev won a silver medal. (Abdullayev was to go on to win a gold medal at the Olympic Games in 2000.)

Indeed, wrestling has been Azerbaijan's most successful sport in Olympic competition. From the 1996 games to the 2016 Olympics, the country's wrestlers had won a total of 22 medals, including 4 golds. Its next best sport has been boxing, in which eight medals were won during those games. The remainder of its medals were won in judo (four), shooting (three), taekwondo (three), and canoeing (two) for a total of 42 medals. Seven of the medal-winning athletes were women.

Azerbaijan has sent far fewer athletes to the Winter Olympics, and as of 2020, there have been no medal winners.

INTERNET LINKS

https://www.azernews.az/culture/49831.html
The Azerbaijani tea tradition is explained in detail.

https://ich.unesco.org/en/USL/chovqan-a-traditional-karabakh-horse-riding-game-in-the-republic-of-azerbaijan-00905
The UNESCO listing for chovqan includes an excellent video.

https://theculturetrip.com/europe/azerbaijan/articles/chovgan-azerbaijans-thrilling-national-sport/
This article provides an explanation of chovqan.

FESTIVALS

A building in Baku is decorated for the springtime festival of Nowruz.

12

I N AZERBAIJAN, THE NEW YEAR BEGINS on January 1, as it does almost everywhere else in the world. That is, everywhere that uses the Gregorian, or Western, calendar. Even though it is nearly universal, at least for civil purposes, it is not the only calendar of importance. Muslims, for example, follow the Islamic lunar calendar for religious festivals, which is why those dates are changeable on the Western calendar.

In Azerbaijan, they also observe the Iranian, or Persian, calendar for certain cultural purposes. In neighboring Iran, it is the official calendar, and it is one of the longest chronological calendars in human history. This calendar begins the new year on the vernal, or spring, equinox. This usually falls on March 20 or 21, and therefore the corresponding new year's festival, Nowruz—which means "new day" in Persian—falls on the same day.

NOWRUZ

The springtime festival grew out of ancient, pre-Islamic, Zoroastrian religious traditions. Today, it is observed by more than 300 million people of various nationalities across western and central Asia, the Balkans, the Middle East, and the Caucasus region. There are many variations of the

In 2009, the spring festival of Nowruz was added to the UNESCO Intangible Cultural Heritage of Humanity list. And in 2010, Azerbaijan was one of several United Nations member countries to introduce a resolution proclaiming March 21 as International Day of Nowruz, a part of the UN's "culture of peace."

A Nowruz table is an opulent display of traditional items. Here, special pastries, sweets, and candles surround a centerpiece of newly sprouted greens.

festival's name, and in Azerbaijan, it is known as Nowruz Bayrami, or simply Nowruz. For most celebrants, the holiday is now a secular occasion, rich with colorful, symbolic customs and food traditions.

In Azerbaijan, Nowruz is observed as a national holiday, and workers and schoolchildren receive five days off. This is a traditional time for families to be together. They prepare for the holiday by spring-cleaning their homes, tending to the graves of their ancestors, planting trees, painting eggs, and baking special pastries.

Customs include celebrations of the four elements—earth, wind, fire, and water. For example, people symbolically cleanse their souls by jumping over bonfires and lighting candles. Wheat is sprouted to welcome the new growing season. A large copper tray bearing a display of sprouted wheat and colored eggs is a traditional centerpiece on the feast table. Special songs, dances, and games add to the festivities.

RELIGIOUS FESTS

Islamic celebrations run the emotional gamut from joyful to solemn to tragic or dramatic. The two most important religious feasts are Eid al-Adha and Eid al-Fitr, which are dated according to the Islamic calendar and therefore fall on a different date each year on the Western calendar.

EID AL-ADHA   Also called Gurban Bayrami, the Festival of the Sacrifice is Islam's most sacred holy day of the year. It celebrates the biblical prophet Ibrahim (Abraham), who, in a test of faith, was willing to sacrifice his son in obedience to God's command. At the last second, God spared his son to be

Sheep are for sale on a city street in advance of the Eid al-Adha festival.

January 1–2   New Year's Day
January 20   Martyrs' Day
March 8   International Women's Day
March 20–24   Nowruz
May 9   Victory Day
May 28   Republic Day
June 15   National Salvation Day
June 26   Armed Forces Day
November 9   Flag Day
December 31   Solidarity Day
Changeable   Eid al-Adha (Feast of the Sacrifice)
                Eid al-Fitr (end of Ramadan)

replaced with a goat or sheep. This story is from the Old Testament, a biblical text honored by Muslims as much as by Jews and Christians.

The festival lasts three days. It coincides with the end of the traditional hajj pilgrimage to Mecca. Azeri families celebrate the festival, especially in rural areas, by ritually slaughtering a sheep or a goat. Meat from the animal, a symbol of patriarch Ibrahim's faith in Allah, is then given to the poor and also shared among friends and family, becoming the basis for a great feast.

ASHURA This day is observed throughout all Islam but for different reasons and in different ways. Among Sunni Muslims, it is a minor occasion commemorating the biblical day when God parted the Red Sea for Moses and his followers to escape from the armies of the Egyptian pharaoh. However, for Shia Muslims—the great majority of Azerbaijanis—it is an especially holy occasion marking a more somber event.

Ashura is a commemoration of the martyrdom of Husayn ibn Ali, a grandson of the Prophet Muhammad. He was killed at the Battle of Karbala, in modern-day Iraq, in 680 CE. According to Islamic history, Husayn and his family were traveling to Al-Kufa, where he expected to be crowned caliph, or leader. Instead, he was met by an opposition army. In a brief battle, Husayn and all his followers were killed. This event prompted the establishment of the Shia sect and led to the resulting schism between the two branches of Islam.

Many Shia will dress in black and offer prayers of mourning for Husayn ibn Ali. However, among the very pious—a small but growing minority in Azerbaijan—Ashura is a time for public demonstrations of intense grief. These faithful carry out acts of lamentation, such as weeping and chest beating. Some men whip themselves with chains or sharp objects in remembrance of Husayn's suffering, and these rituals can be quite bloody.

A child prays with her family during Ashura in Baku.

Azerbaijanis who take a more progressive view tend to object to these demonstrations, finding them appalling and primitive. In lieu of self-flagellation, the Azerbaijani government has suggested donating blood to blood banks as a more modern way of commemorating the event.

RAMADAN This month-long fast occurs in the ninth month of the Islamic calendar. It is a time for solemn reflection, prayer, and spirituality. During Ramadan, Muslims are to refrain from eating, drinking, smoking, and other physical pleasures from dawn to dusk. The elderly, sick, or pregnant are exempt from this fast.

EID AL-FITR At the end of Ramadan, people celebrate the next three days with the "feast of the breaking of the fast," Eid al-Fitr. Joyful people wear their best clothes, wish their neighbors a "Blessed Eid," and attend prayer services. After that, families and friends gather for great feasts with special foods, sweets, and presents for children.

PATRIOTIC CELEBRATIONS

As in most nations, there are several patriotic holidays in Azerbaijan, which are occasions for demonstrating national pride. These gatherings feature marching bands, waving flags, military displays, and speeches.

Children in national costumes perform a dance at a festival in Baku.

The great pride the Azerbaijani people feel in their independent republic is evident on these days. Some of these holidays celebrate the country's first brief episode of independence. Republic Day, for example, honors the founding of the first Azerbaijani Democratic Republic in 1918, and Armed Forces Day celebrates the creation of the republic's first army in the same year.

Other patriotic days commemorate declaring independence in 1991 and establishing the new republic. National Revival Day (which is an observance but not a national holiday) on November 17 marks the first anti-Soviet uprising in 1988. More than two years of uprisings and repression followed. One marker on the road to independence came in 1989, when Azerbaijanis and Iranians tore down the border fences the Soviets had put up between the two countries to prevent the Iranian Azerbaijanis from joining the northern Azeris. This event is celebrated as Solidarity Day on December 31 each year.

Soviet repression is marked by Martyrs' Day, on January 20. This is a tribute to civilians in Baku who were gunned down by Soviet troops in 1990. October 18 celebrates National Independence Day, marking the day in 1991 when the parliament announced the dissolution of the Soviet Union and Azerbaijan began its second democratic republic.

After declaring independence, the new government was not able to settle the bitter warfare with Armenians over Nagorno-Karabakh. In 1993, Heydar Aliyev took advantage of the chaos and was named president. On June 15, parliament officially asked Aliyev to lead the country, a date that is now celebrated as National Salvation Day. Constitution Day (November 12) commemorates the adoption of the republic's new constitution in 1995.

OTHER FESTIVALS

Possibly the largest annual event in Azerbaijan is the Caspian Oil and Gas Exhibition and Conference. Held in late May or early June in and around Baku, this week-long event brings national leaders and around 10,000 oil industry professionals together from all over the world. It has become a festive celebration of Azerbaijan's potential as one of the great producers of oil and natural gas.

The capital city is also the site of the International Baku Jazz Festival, which began in 2005, and various other music and art festivals as well. Outside of Baku, there's a Pomegranate Festival in Goychay, which usually takes place in October, the Quba Apple Festival in the city of that name, and numerous other food fests.

INTERNET LINKS

https://eurasianet.org/azerbaijani-shias-gather-for-ashura-under-close-watch-from-the-state
This article looks at the ways Ashura is observed in Azerbaijan.

https://www.timeanddate.com/holidays/azerbaijan
This calendar site lists the annual holidays and observances in Azerbaijan.

http://unesco.preslib.az/en/page/zOSIRFONXy
This UNESCO page describes the Nowruz holiday in Azerbaijan.

FOOD

Traditional flatbread is baked in a tandor oven. The dough is stuck to the sides of the pit, where it bakes from the heat of the embers.

13

A ZERBAIJANI CUISINE REFLECTS THE country's history, ethnic and religious background, and geographical location. The region's array of climatic zones supports different crops. Colder regions, for example, provide grapes and many kinds of nuts as well as staples such as wheat and barley. Subtropical areas produce pomegranates and citrus fruit.

The Azerbaijani people are also very creative in their use of herbs and spices to vary standard dishes. Their cuisine shares many of the same foods, flavors, and methods as Persian, Caucasian, and Russian food traditions. Distinctive flavors are achieved with herbs including fresh mint, coriander, dill, basil, and parsley, and spices such as sumac, cumin, saffron, and cinnamon. A wide variety of dried fruits, such as apricots, plums, dates, and raisins, is enjoyed in savory as well as sweet dishes.

THE SOVIET INFLUENCE

During Azerbaijan's 70 years as one of the 15 Soviet republics, the central government in Moscow had a strong influence on the foods the Azerbaijanis ate and produced. Soviet planners hoped to transform the many nationalities and cultures that made up its vast empire into a single efficient system. Each republic or province would contribute one or more important products to the national economy. Azerbaijan, for instance, was a major oil producer, and its farms provided slightly more than 10 percent

Flatbreads are baked throughout the Caucasus and central Asia in much the same way they have been for thousands of years. They differ from region to region in size, shape, and thickness, as well as in the type of wheat used to make the flour. Traditional flatbreads are cooked in a tandor–a clay or stone oven pit in the ground–or on special metal pans placed on open fires.

of the fruit and vegetables needed for the entire Soviet Union. Other republics in turn sent certain products to Azerbaijan: butter came from Russia, poultry from Hungary, condensed milk from the Ukraine, and cheese from Bulgaria.

Another way that communist planners influenced national cuisine was by encouraging people to follow a typical Russian diet. Throughout Azerbaijan, workers in factories and government offices and students in universities and vocational schools all ate in large, government-operated cafés. The food was somewhat bland, but it was wholesome and free. While a few national dishes, such as lamb kebabs, were served, the menu emphasized traditional Russian foods, such as goulash, meat cutlets, *shi* (fish soup), and borscht. This seemed to be part of the plan to forge a single, united Soviet people.

Even today, several decades after Azerbaijan gained its independence, many traditional Russian dishes have become part of the emerging Azerbaijani cuisine. A basic Russian salad, for example, made of beans, potatoes, carrots, pickled beets, and cabbage, is now standard in many Azerbaijani homes. Another Russian dish is called *stolichniy salat*; it is basically a potato salad with shredded chicken, carrots, and peas, topped with a mayonnaise-like dressing. This has become a popular first dish at weddings and other large functions.

Another holdover from the Soviet era is Russian vodka, which is much loved in this country. This is a curious paradox, given that as Muslims, Azerbaijanis are forbidden by their religion from drinking alcohol. When history forces clashing cultures to mix, contradictions can become customary.

While some aspects of the old Soviet regime may hang on, Azerbaijan now promotes its own cuisine as a national culinary heritage to relish and preserve.

MEATS

Being a Muslim people, most Azerbaijanis do not eat pork, as it is forbidden by Islamic law. Lamb is the most common meat, but beef, chicken, and fish are also consumed. Meat is served in a variety of ways, mostly grilled as kebabs, minced and mixed with rice, or stewed.

Kebabs are often referred to by the Russian word *shashlik*, meaning "sword" or skewer. The standard kebab consists of chunks of marinated meat threaded onto a skewer and grilled over the embers. Vegetables are usually grilled on a separate skewer. Lamb kebabs are very common. *Lyulya*, or *lule*, kebab is made of chopped meat, spices, and herbs that are shaped into sausage shapes and grilled on skewers. Sometimes it is served with lavash bread wrapped around it.

While lamb kebabs are the most popular meat dish, there are other specialties in Azerbaijan. *Balig* is a popular fish dish. The fish, usually sturgeon, is cut into chunks and grilled as a kebab. It is served with a tangy sour-plum sauce. *Lavangi* is a roast chicken stuffed with walnuts and herbs and then baked in an earthenware casserole. It is a specialty of the Talysh.

TRADITIONAL DISHES

A typical breakfast features tea with jams, soft white cheese, honey, sweet butter, and bread. Scrambled eggs with herbs, called *kuku*, are also often served at the morning meal. For other meals, soups, stews, stuffed vegetables, and rice dishes are traditional.

A man grills lamb kebabs in Goychay.

DOLMA   There are several varieties of dolma, or stuffed vegetables. The basic recipe consists of minced lamb mixed with rice and flavored with mint, fennel, and cinnamon. The mixture is then wrapped in grape leaves to make *yarpaq dolmasi* or wrapped in cabbage leaves to make *kalam dolmasi*. That filling, or something similar, is also used to stuff tomatoes, green peppers, or eggplants. "Dolma making and sharing tradition, a marker of cultural identity" in Azerbaijan was added to the UNESCO Intangible Cultural Heritage (ICH) list in 2017.

SOUPS AND STEWS   Azeris are fond of hot and cold soups, including dishes that are thick enough to be called stews. *Dovga*, for example, is a hot, thick

A *shah plov* is a crown-shaped dish of rice pilaf, prepared with dried fruits, such as apricots and raisins, and minced lamb. The "crown" is made of thin flatbread.

soup made of yogurt, rice, spinach, and fennel. *Dograma* is a cold soup of sour milk, potato, onion, and cucumber. *Kufta bozbash* is a hot soup made with meatballs, potatoes, and peas boiled in broth with saffron and turmeric. The large, hearty meatballs are made of minced lamb and rice and may have a dried plum inside. *Piti* is more a stew than a soup. It is made of lamb, chickpeas, and saffron. Like many Azeri dishes, piti is cooked and served in individual earthenware crocks. *Dushbara* is a classic dish consisting of small, ravioli-size dumplings stuffed with minced lamb and herbs, served in a hot broth.

PLOV   This dish is a pilaf of rice and meat. One of the most typical versions consists of lamb, rice, chopped onion, and prunes. Saffron and cinnamon are added to this flavorful dish, which is commonly made at home. *Shah plov*

("plov for a king") is made for special occasions; it's a dish of lamb, rice, dried fruits, and nuts encased in a bread-covered ring or crown.

A woman makes *qutab*, a flatbread stuffed with minced greens.

BREADS

Most Azerbaijani breads are flatbreads of varying thicknesses. Tandor bread is a puffy, pita-style bread cooked in a clay oven called a tandor. Lavash is a soft, very thin, unleavened bread cooked in a tandor or on another very hot surface. The traditional making of lavash has been designated as a piece of Intangible Cultural Heritage shared by Azerbaijan, Iran, Kazakhstan, Kyrgyzstan, and Turkey. Lavash is typically served with kebabs or wrapped around kebab meat. Another national dish is called *qutab* (or kutab)—a thin crepe- or pancake-type bread dough that is grilled, stuffed with cheese, meat, or greens, and served with an herbed yogurt sauce.

DESSERTS

Many Azerbaijanis love sweets. They enjoy a wide variety of pastries, which often incorporate ground or finely chopped nuts. For example, *pakhlava* is very popular in Azerbaijan. It's a close cousin to the Middle Eastern pastry called baklava, which is prepared in many versions throughout the Caucasus. Both are sweet, moist pastries of thin, flaky dough layered with spiced ground nuts—usually walnuts, almonds, or hazelnuts—soaked in a honey syrup and cut into diamond shapes. In Azerbaijan, this dessert is traditionally served during the spring holiday of Nowruz. Another pastry is *shekerbura*, a crescent-shaped turnover filled with sweetened, cardamom-spiced ground nuts.

Firmi is a kind of rice pudding. Nogul is a candy made with cilantro or cardamom seeds boiled in a sugar syrup, and halva is a dense confection— something like fudge, but with an entirely different flavor — based on tahini,

Pakhlava is a popular sweet pastry of nuts and honey.

or sesame paste. There are also many kinds of cookies and buns that are perfect for enjoying with a cup of tea.

TEA TIME

In fact, tea is the preferred beverage in Azerbaijan; it's served throughout the day, at teahouses and at home. It's always offered to guests as a sign of hospitality—according to tradition, one should never allow a guest to leave the house without at least one cup of tea.

Hot black tea is served in small, pear-shaped glasses and may be served with lemon and sugar cubes but never with milk. Tea is often served with thick, chunky jams. The diner can place a small spoonful of jam in his or her mouth and sip the hot tea through it. The jam flavors the tea and provides a bit of chewiness. The same can be done with a sugar cube.

INTERNET LINKS

http://flavorsofbaku.com
The recipe site features the dishes of Azerbaijan and other related cultures.

https://ich.unesco.org/en/RL/dolma-making-and-sharing-tradition-a-marker-of-cultural-identity-01188
https://ich.unesco.org/en/RL/flatbread-making-and-sharing-culture-lavash-katyrma-jupka-yufka-01181
The ICH listings for dolma and lavash are presented on these pages.

https://www.saveur.com/azerbaijan-baku-cuisine
This article explores the flavors of Baku.

https://theculturetrip.com/europe/azerbaijan/articles/the-20-best-dishes-in-azerbaijan
This travel site offers photos and descriptions of the country's most iconic foods.

LYULYA KEBAB (AZERBAIJANI GROUND LAMB KEBAB)

2 pounds (approx. 1 kg)
  ground lamb
2 medium onions, peeled
  and grated
4 cloves of garlic,
  finely chopped
¼ cup fresh cilantro or parsley,
  finely chopped
1 teaspoon cumin
2 teaspoons dried mint
½ teaspoon cayenne pepper
1 teaspoon paprika
Salt, pepper to taste

Place the ground lamb in a large mixing bowl.

In a small bowl, combine the grated onion, garlic, herbs, and spices. Add to the lamb, and knead gently with the fingers until mixture is well combined. At this point, the meat mixture can be refrigerated overnight to develop flavor, but it's not necessary

Shape the lamb mixture onto skewers, making long sausage shapes. Flat skewers work best at keeping the meat from spinning.

Preheat the grill to medium heat. Grill the kebabs until browned on one side, then turn and repeat until just cooked through. Do not overcook or the meat can get dry.

Serve hot with flatbread, plain yogurt, and vegetables such as tomatoes, cucumbers, and peppers. Serves six.

SHEKERBURA

These crescent turnovers are traditional for Nowruz, the spring holiday. Authentic shekerbura are decorated with designs made with special tools, but they can be left plain. Many recipes call for a yeasted, sour cream dough; this one is simplified.

For the dough:
2 cups flour
½ cup cold unsalted butter, cut into
  small pieces
1 egg , slightly beaten
¼ cup cold water

For the filling:
1¼ cup almond meal or finely
  ground almonds
⅓ cup sugar
¼ teaspoon ground cardamom

Prepare the dough: Attach a paddle attachment to a stand mixer. Place the flour, butter, egg, and water in the bowl, and mix until a smooth dough comes together. (Alternatively, use a food processor, or mix by hand.)

Shape the dough into a long rope. Divide it into 15 pieces of equal size (about 1 ounce per piece). Form balls and flatten them slightly. Place them, well spaced, on a baking sheet lined with parchment paper. Cover with plastic wrap. Refrigerate for one to two hours.

Preheat oven to 350°F (177°C). Meanwhile, prepare the filling: In a medium bowl, mix together the almond meal, sugar, and cardamom until well combined.

Roll each piece of dough into a circle about 4 inches (10 cm) in diameter (not too thin).

In the center of each circle, add a tablespoon of filling. Close the circle in half. Pinch the edges to seal them. Then crimp the edge more tightly, folding inward. If desired, use a fork, small knife, or another tool to etch zigzag geometric patterns on the dough, taking care not to cut through it.

Place turnovers on parchment-covered baking sheet. Bake for 20 to 25 minutes. Let cool. If turnovers are undecorated, sprinkle lightly with confectioner's sugar.

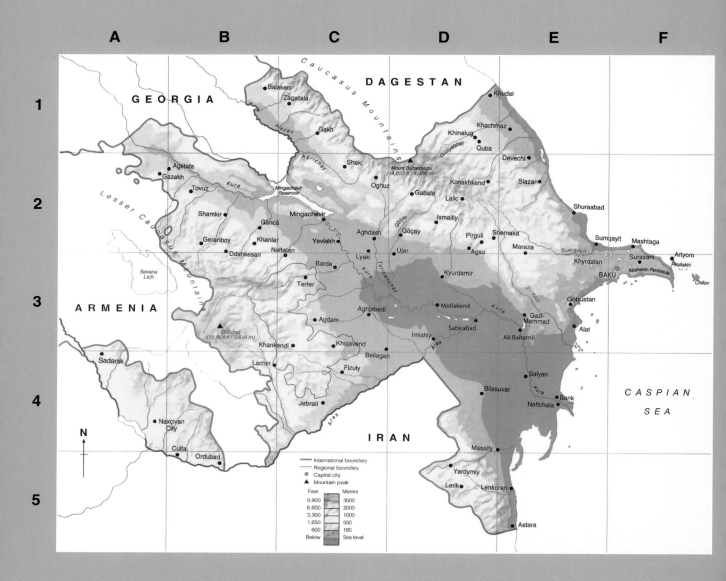

Absheron
  Peninsula, F3
Agdam, C3
Aghdash, C2
Aghjabedi, C3
Agstafa, B2
Agsu, D2
Alat, E3
Ali Bairamli, E3
Aras (river), A4,
  A5, B5, C4—C5,
  D3—D4
Artyom, F3
Astara, E5

Baku, F3
Balaken, B1
Bank, E4
Barda, C3
Bellagan, C3
Bilasuvar, D4

Caspian Sea, D1,
  E1—E5, F1—F5
Chilov (island), F3
Culfa, B5

Dälidag, B3
Ddshkesan, B2
Devechi, E2

Fizuly, C4

Gabala, D2
Gakh, C1
Ganca, B2
Gazi-Mammad, E3
Geranboy, B2
Gobustan, E3
Gocay, D2

lmishly, D3
lsmailly, D2

Jebrail, C4

Khachmaz, E1
Khankendi, C3
Khanlar, B2
Khinalug, D1
Khojavend, C3
Khudat, D1
Konakhkend, D2
Kura (river), C2, C3,
  D3, E3, E4
Kyurdamir, D3

Lachin, B4
Lalic, D2
Lenkoran, E5
Lerik, D5
Lyaki, C2

Maraza, E2
Masally, D4

Mashtaga, F2
Mingachevir, C2
Mollakend, D3
Mount Bazardyuzu,
  D2

Naftalan, C3
Naxcivan City, A4
Neftchala, E4

Oghuz, C2
Ordubad, B5

Pirallakhi (island),
  F3
Pirguli, D2

Quba, D1

Sadarak, A4
Salyan, E4
Shamkir, B2
Sheki, C2
Shemaka, D2
Shuraabad, E2
Siazan, E2
Sumqayit, E2
Suraxani, F3

Terter, C3
Tovuz, B2

Ujar, D3

Yardymly, D5
Yevlakh, C2

Zagatala, C1

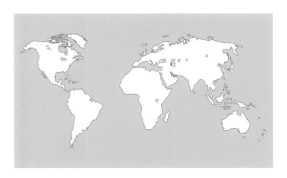

ECONOMIC AZERBAIJAN

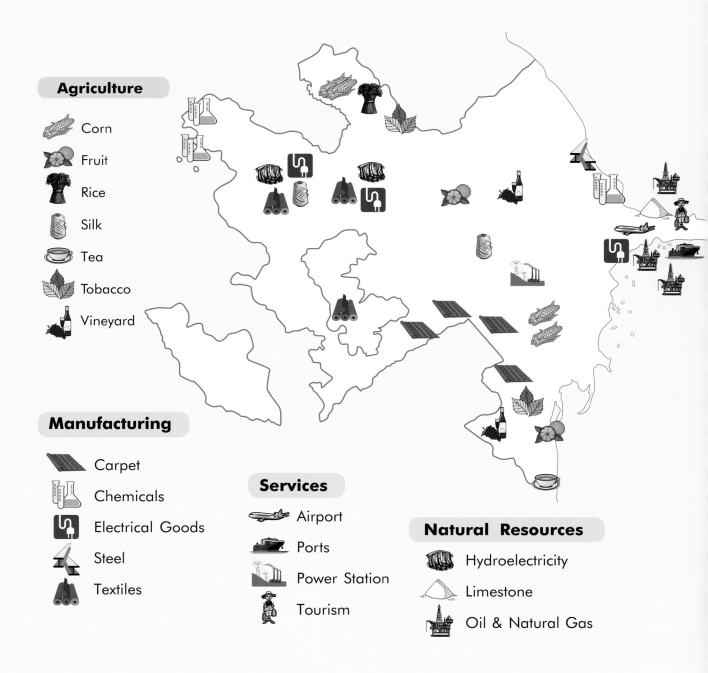

Agriculture

- Corn
- Fruit
- Rice
- Silk
- Tea
- Tobacco
- Vineyard

Manufacturing

- Carpet
- Chemicals
- Electrical Goods
- Steel
- Textiles

Services

- Airport
- Ports
- Power Station
- Tourism

Natural Resources

- Hydroelectricity
- Limestone
- Oil & Natural Gas

ABOUT THE ECONOMY

All figures are 2017 estimates, unless otherwise noted.

GROSS DOMESTIC PRODUCT (OFFICIAL EXCHANGE RATE)
$40.67 billion

GDP PER CAPITA
$17,500

GDP GROWTH
0.1 percent

GDP COMPOSITION, BY SECTOR OF ORIGIN
agriculture: 6.1 percent
industry: 53.5 percent
services: 40.4 percent

NATURAL RESOURCES
petroleum, natural gas, iron ore, nonferrous metals, bauxite

CURRENCY
Azerbaijani manat (AZN)
$1US dollar = 1.70 Azerbaijani manat
(February 2020)

AGRICULTURAL PRODUCTS
fruit, vegetables, grain, rice, grapes, tea, cotton, tobacco, cattle, pigs, sheep, goats

INDUSTRIES
petroleum and petroleum products, natural gas, oil field equipment, steel, iron ore, cement, chemicals and petrochemicals, textiles

MAJOR EXPORTS
oil and gas, machinery, foodstuffs, cotton

MAJOR IMPORTS
machinery and equipment, foodstuffs, metals, chemicals

MAIN TRADE PARTNERS
Italy, Russia, Turkey, China, United States, Israel, Ukraine, Germany, Czech Republic, Georgia

LABOR FORCE
5.12 million

LABOR FORCE BY OCCUPATION
agriculture: 37 percent
industry: 14.3 percent
services: 48.9 percent (2014)

UNEMPLOYMENT RATE
5 percent

POPULATION BELOW POVERTY LINE
4.9 percent (2015)

INFLATION RATE
13 percent

CULTURAL AZERBAIJAN

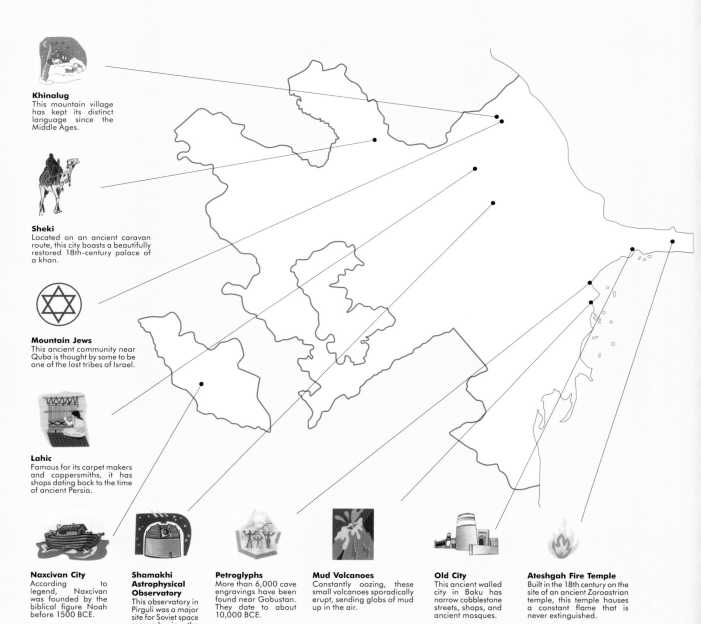

Khinalug
This mountain village has kept its distinct language since the Middle Ages.

Sheki
Located on an ancient caravan route, this city boasts a beautifully restored 18th-century palace of a khan.

Mountain Jews
This ancient community near Quba is thought by some to be one of the lost tribes of Israel.

Lahic
Famous for its carpet makers and coppersmiths, it has shops dating back to the time of ancient Persia.

Naxcivan City
According to legend, Naxcivan was founded by the biblical figure Noah before 1500 BCE.

Shamakhi Astrophysical Observatory
This observatory in Pirguli was a major site for Soviet space research in the 1960s and 1970s.

Petroglyphs
More than 6,000 cave engravings have been found near Gobustan. They date to about 10,000 BCE.

Mud Volcanoes
Constantly oozing, these small volcanoes sporadically erupt, sending globs of mud up in the air.

Old City
This ancient walled city in Baku has narrow cobblestone streets, shops, and ancient mosques.

Ateshgah Fire Temple
Built in the 18th century on the site of an ancient Zoroastrian temple, this temple houses a constant flame that is never extinguished.

ABOUT THE CULTURE

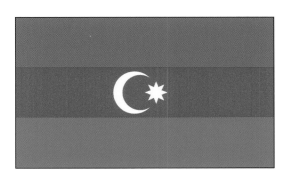

All figures are 2020 estimates unless otherwise noted.

OFFICIAL NAME
Republic of Azerbaijan

GOVERNMENT TYPE
presidential republic

TOTAL AREA
33,436.5 square miles (86,600 sq km)

CAPITAL
Baku

POPULATION
10,205,810 (July 2020)

POPULATION GROWTH RATE
0.77 percent

URBANIZATION
urban population: 56.4 percent of total population

ETHNIC GROUPS
Azerbaijani 91.6 percent, Lezgin 2 percent, Russian 1.3 percent, Armenian 1.3 percent, Talysh 1.3 percent, other 2.4 percent (2009) *Note: The separatist Nagorno-Karabakh region is populated almost entirely by ethnic Armenians.*

RELIGIONS
Muslim 96.9 percent (predominantly Shia), Christian 3 percent, other <0.1, unaffiliated <0.1 (2010)
Note: Religious affiliation for the majority of Azerbaijanis is largely nominal; percentages for actual practicing adherents are probably much lower.

MAIN LANGUAGES
Azerbaijani (Azeri) (official) 92.5 percent, Russian 1.4 percent, Armenian 1.4 percent, other 4.7 percent (2009)

LIFE EXPECTANCY AT BIRTH
total population: 73.6 years
male: 70.5 years
female: 76.9 years

TIMELINE

IN AZERBAIJAN	IN THE WORLD
	117 CE The Roman Empire reaches its greatest extent
300–400 CE Arabs conquer Central Asia.	**600** The Maya civilization reaches its height.
642 Caucasian Albania becomes Muslim.	**1000** The Chinese perfect gunpowder and begin to use it in warfare.
1110–1200 Seljuk Turkish dynasty rule takes place.	
1236–1498 Mongols under Genghis Khan control Azerbaijan.	
1500 With the Safavid dynasty in power, Shia Islam is established in this region.	**1620** Pilgrims sail the *Mayflower* to America.
1722 Safavid rule ends; Azerbaijan is splintered into several khanates.	**1776** The U.S. Declaration of Independence is adopted.
	1789–1799 The French Revolution takes place.
1804–1828 The Russo-Persian Wars take place. Russia controls Azerbaijan north of Aras River.	**1861** The American Civil War begins.
1870–1915 The oil industry makes Baku a boomtown.	**1869** The Suez Canal opens.
	1914–1918 World War I takes place.
1918 Azerbaijan forms an independent republic.	
1920s Azerbaijan becomes part of the Soviet Union.	
1930s Communist purges are ordered by Soviet dictator Joseph Stalin.	**1939–1945** World War II devastates Europe.
	1966–1969 The Chinese Cultural Revolution takes place.
	1969 U.S. astronaut Neil Armstrong becomes the first human on the moon.

IN AZERBAIJAN	IN THE WORLD
1991	**1991**
Azerbaijan declares independence from the Soviet Union.	The Soviet Union breaks up.
1992	
War takes places in Nagorno-Karabakh.	
1993	
Heydar Aliyev becomes president.	
1994	
Aliyev signs a cease-fire with Armenia.	**1997**
	Great Britain returns Hong Kong to China.
2001	**2001**
Azerbaijan officially shifts to the Latin alphabet.	Terrorists attack the United States on September 11.
2003	**2003**
Ilham Aliyev becomes president; Heydar Aliyev dies.	The Iraq War begins.
2006	
The South Caucasus Pipeline, which runs from Azerbaijan to Turkey, starts pumping natural gas.	
2008	**2008**
Ilham Aliyev wins a second term as president in an election boycotted by the main opposition parties.	The United States elects its first African American president, Barack Obama.
2009	**2009**
A referendum approves constitutional changes that remove a ban on presidential term limits, allowing a third term for President Ilham Aliyev.	An outbreak of H1N1 flu takes place around the world.
2016	**2015–2016**
Dozens are killed in a flare-up of fighting in the enclave of Nagorno-Karabakh.	ISIS launches terror attacks in Belgium and France.
2017	**2017**
Azerbaijan denies reports of a secret slush fund, the "Azerbaijan Laundromat," for paying off European politicians and laundering money.	Donald Trump becomes U.S. president.
2018	
Heydar Aliyev wins fourth term as president; he appoints his wife, Mehriban, as first vice president.	**2019**
	Notre Dame Cathedral in Paris is damaged by fire. Donald Trump is impeached.
2020	**2020**
Renewed fighting breaks out between Armenians and Azerbaijanis.	A coronavirus pandemic spreads across the world.

GLOSSARY

ashug
A poet-singer in the tradition of strolling minstrels; popular since the Middle Ages.

Besbarmaq Dag
Five-Finger Mountain, a place where religious mystics pray and dispense wisdom to their followers.

caviar
The roe of Caspian Sea sturgeons; one of the world's most prized delicacies.

chovqan
A traditional game like polo played on horseback.

Icari Sahar
The walled Old Town of Baku.

khanate
An area or province ruled by a khan.

Quran
The holy book of Islam.

lesginka
A popular folk dance from the Lezghian peoples of the northern mountains of Azerbaijan.

madrassa
An Islamic center of learning.

mugam
A musical style. Also, a trio of musicians that plays in that style.

nard
A hugely popular board game; also known as backgammon.

Pan-Azerbaijani movement
A movement with the aim to unite the northern and southern branches of the Azerbaijani people.

Ramadan
The holiest month in the Islamic calendar. Observant Muslims fast during daylight hours during this month.

shashlik
An Azeri kebab; literally, "sword," in Russian.

zakat
A tax to support the poor; paying this tax is one of the Five Pillars of Islam.

FOR FURTHER INFORMATION

BOOKS

Amiraslanov, Tahir, and Leyla Rahmanova. *The Azerbaijani Kitchen: A Cookbook*. London, UK: Saqi Books, 2014.

Kazimova, Nikki. *Azerbaijan—Culture Smart!: The Essential Guide to Customs & Culture.* London, UK: Kuperard, 2011.

Lutterbeck, Barbara, ed. *Azerbaijan: Culture and Cuisine*. Cologne, Germany: Wienand Verlag, 2016.

ONLINE

AzerNews. https://www.azernews.az.

BBC News. "Azerbaijan Country Profile." https://www.bbc.com/news/world-europe-17043424.

BBC News. "Timeline: Ajerbaijan." http://news.bbc.co.uk/2/hi/europe/country_profiles/1235740.stm.

CIA. *The World Factbook*. "Azerbaijan." https://www.cia.gov/library/publications/the-world-factbook/geos/aj.html.

Consulate General of the Republic of Azerbaijan. https://www.azconsulatela.org/.

Culture Trip. "Azerbaijan." https://theculturetrip.com/asia/azerbaijan.

Encyclopædia Britannica. "Azerbaijan." https://www.britannica.com/place/Azerbaijan.

Eurasianet. https://eurasianet.org/region/azerbaijan.

MUSIC

Azerbaijan: Traditional Music. Lok-Batan Folklore Group. ARC Music, 2011.

The Land of Fire: Music of Azerbaijan. Various artists. FM Records, 2010.

FILM

Baku: The City of Ali and Nino. Directed by Teresa Cherfas. Journeyman Pictures, 2016.

Zaha Hadid. Directed by Carine Roy. Yuyu, 2016.

BIBLIOGRAPHY

BBC News. "Azerbaijan Country Profile." https://www.bbc.com/news/world-europe-17043424.

BBC News. "Timeline: Ajerbaijan." http://news.bbc.co.uk/2/hi/europe/country_profiles/1235740.stm.

Bremzen, Anya von. "The World's Last Great Undiscovered Cuisine." *Saveur*, January 30, 2017. https://www.saveur.com/azerbaijan-baku-cuisine.

CIA. *The World Factbook*. "Azerbaijan." https://www.cia.gov/library/publications/the-world-factbook/geos/aj.html.

Encyclopædia Britannica. "Azerbaijan." https://www.britannica.com/place/Azerbaijan.

Foley, Rebeka. "Why Azerbaijan's Dynasty-Building Is a Bad Sign for Europe." Freedom House, March 9, 2017. https://freedomhouse.org/article/why-azerbaijans-dynasty-building-bad-sign-europe.

Freedom House. "Freedom in the World 2020." https://freedomhouse.org/country/azerbaijan/freedom-world/2020.

Mamedov, Eldar. "Azerbaijan: Examining the Source of Discontent in Nardaran." *Eurasianet*, December 8, 2015. https://eurasianet.org/azerbaijan-examining-the-source-of-discontent-in-nardaran.

Morgans, Julian. "This City of Oil Rigs Is Collapsing Into the Caspian Sea." *Vice*, February 11, 2018. https://www.vice.com/en_au/article/7x784g/this-city-of-oil-rigs-is-collapsing-into-the-caspian-sea.

President of the Republic of Azerbaijan. "Ilham Aliyev chaired meeting on results of 2019." January 13, 2020. https://en.president.az/articles/35601.

Rzayeva, Kamilla. "Azerbaijan's Secret to Long Life? Mountain Air." *CNN Travel*, December 2019. https://www.cnn.com/travel/article/long-life-lerik-azerbaijan-wellness/index.html.

Schoenfeld, Bruce. "This Ancient Silk Road City Is Now a Modern Marvel." *National Geographic,* April 9, 2018. https://www.nationalgeographic.com/travel/destinations/asia/azerbaijan/photos-pictures-baku/.

UNECE. "Azerbaijan presents National Forestry Programme for 2020-2030." https://www.unece.org/info/media/news/forestry-and-timber/2019/azerbaijan-presents-national-forestry-programme-for-2020-2030/doc.html.

UNESCO Intangible Cultural Heritage, Azerbaijan. https://ich.unesco.org/en/state/azerbaijan-AZ.

UNESCO World Heritage Centre, Azerbaijan. https://whc.unesco.org/en/statesparties/az.

INDEX

INDEX